Contents

KU-467-184

Studying Japan's past

All human beings need food and shelter to survive. They also need a system of beliefs to give shape and meaning to their lives. Throughout history, people have found different ways of meeting these basic needs. By studying the people of Japan, we learn how they created a way of life that sustained them, physically and spiritually.

IN THIS BOOK, we look at four different periods of Japanese history, each one telling us something new about the Japanese way of life and character. We know how people lived during these times through the writings and paintings that were made then, and from the work of **historians**.

Each period is represented by a symbol which is used when information refers mainly to that time. Where there is no symbol, it means that the information generally applies to all four periods.

KEY FOR SYMBOLS

- (fan) **Heian** 790-1185
- (swords) **Kamakura** 1185-1333
- (tea bowl) **Muromachi and Momoyama** 1392-1600
- (woodcut) **Edo** 1600-1868

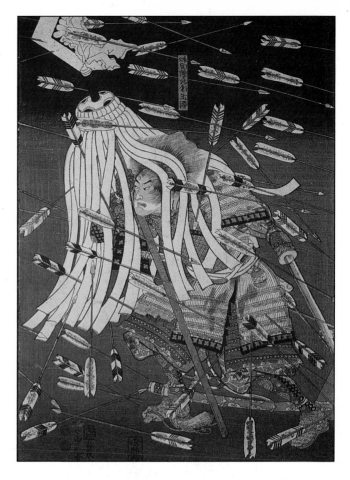

*This print from 1861, 'Last Stand of the Kusunoki Clan', shows a **samurai** warrior in battle dress.*

THE HEIAN PERIOD lasted from about 790 to 1185 and it is called Heian after the city where the emperor lived. This was a time when power was centred around the imperial court. Landowners were very wealthy, but most people in society had very little. During this time, Japanese artists and writers began to throw off the influences of China and find their own identity.

THE KAMAKURA PERIOD lasted from about 1185 to 1333. The court at Heian lost its power to the powerful Minamoto **clan**. The leader of the clan, Yoritomo, established himself as the ruler, or supreme **shogun** of Japan in 1192. A military government called a *bakufu* was set up. Although the emperor kept his court in Kyoto, he had no real **political** power. Yoritomo chose Kamakura as his base because his supporters were mainly samurai warriors from the eastern regions.

Studying old texts, such as 'The Tale of Genji', written in 1010, can help us understand life at that time.

◡ **THE MUROMACHI AND MOMOYAMA** periods lasted from 1392 to 1600. The Kamakura era had ended in confusion, with two emperors and two separate courts. For the next 30 years, the two courts were at war. Eventually, the third shogun of the Muromachi *bakufu*, Yoshimitsu, brought the two courts together and political power was centred in Kyoto. However, the *bakufu* was weak and from 1467 there was a long period of war and unrest. Eventually, Japan was reunified under Toyotomi Hideyoshi. One of the most important cultural features of this time was the rise of **Zen Buddhism** (see page 58).

🐸 **THE EDO PERIOD** began in 1600 and lasted until the beginning of the modern age in 1868. It was named after the city now called Tokyo, where the supreme shogun Tokugawa Ieyasu seized power in 1603. It was a time during which Japan isolated itself from the rest of the world, banning foreigners from entering, and stopping the Japanese from travelling abroad.

◡ *This Zen 'gravel' garden is like a Japanese landscape in miniature.*

Japan's isolation came about because the ruling classes feared invasion by other countries, and the spread of the Christian religion which might unsettle Japan's **class structure** (see page 10). The Edo period was known as 'the great peace'. Popular arts and crafts flourished, particularly the theatre, and people were taught to read and write.

THE MAKE IT WORK! way of looking at history is to ask questions of the past and discover some of the answers by making replicas of the things people made. However, you do not have to make everything in the book to understand the Japanese way of life.

🐸 *A samurai wife wears a fashionable* **kimono** *of the Edo period.*

Timeline

For many centuries Japan was made up of groups of small, independent clans whose chieftains were always at war with each other. In 660 BC, according to legend, a chieftain called Jimmu defeated the other clans and set up his capital on Honshu island. Jimmu, who was believed to be a descendant of the sun goddess, became the first emperor of Japan.

IT TOOK MANY CENTURIES before Japan became anything like a unified country. In AD 710, the city of Nara became Japan's capital (the capital was sited wherever the ruler had his palace, and was usually abandoned after his death). But it was decided that Nara had been built in an unlucky place, so the capital was moved to Heian-kyo in 794. Heian, later known as Kyoto, became the home of the Japanese emperors for over a thousand years. Many old imperial buildings are still there today.

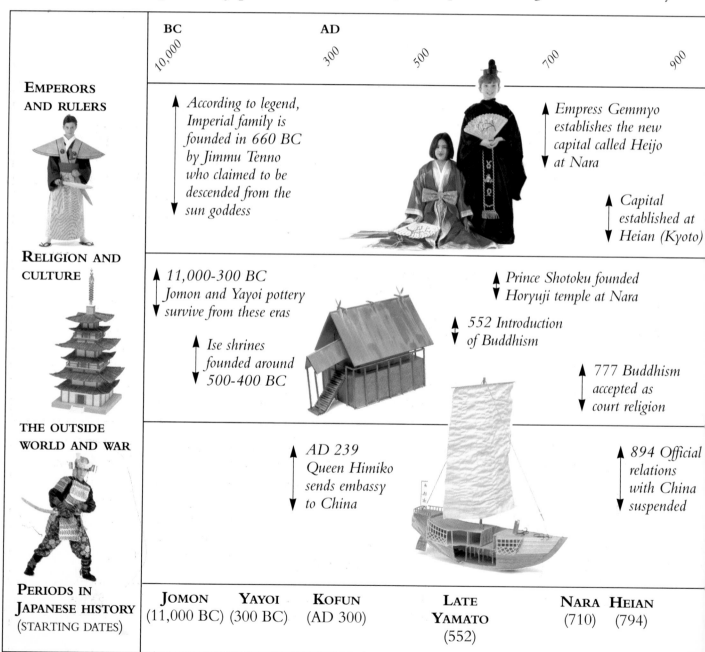

BC | AD
10,000 | 300 | 500 | 700 | 900

EMPERORS AND RULERS

According to legend, Imperial family is founded in 660 BC by Jimmu Tenno who claimed to be descended from the sun goddess

Empress Gemmyo establishes the new capital called Heijo at Nara

Capital established at Heian (Kyoto)

RELIGION AND CULTURE

11,000-300 BC Jomon and Yayoi pottery survive from these eras

Ise shrines founded around 500-400 BC

Prince Shotoku founded Horyuji temple at Nara

552 Introduction of Buddhism

777 Buddhism accepted as court religion

THE OUTSIDE WORLD AND WAR

AD 239 Queen Himiko sends embassy to China

894 Official relations with China suspended

PERIODS IN JAPANESE HISTORY (STARTING DATES)

| JOMON (11,000 BC) | YAYOI (300 BC) | KOFUN (AD 300) | LATE YAMATO (552) | NARA (710) | HEIAN (794) |

THERE WERE LONG STRETCHES of Japanese history when real power was not in the hands of the emperors. From 1190, power passed to the military rulers of Japan, known as shoguns, and this heralded the age of the samurai warrior. Finally, after centuries of war, three warrior leaders emerged who brought peace to Japan. In 1603, Tokugawa Ieyasu became shogun. His capital, Edo, was one of the largest cities in the world at that time, and his family's rule continued for 14 generations, until 1868.

MODERN TIMES in Japan date from July 1853, when four American warships asked for the right of entry to Tokyo Bay, so that trading could take place between Japan and America. Until this time, Japan's rulers had turned down trading requests from foreign governments because they feared invasion and the influence of Christianity. But Japan could no longer survive alone, so entry was granted to the US ships. The emperor was restored to power and the country's first **general election** was held in 1890.

AD

1000   1200   1400   1600   1800

Minamato Yoritomo establishes military government. Samurai rule begins

Oda Nobunaga conquers central Japan. He is killed 14 years later. Toyotomi Hideyoshi succeeds and unifies Japan

Emperor restored to power in 1868. Court moves to Edo (renamed Tokyo)

Tokugawa Ieyasu takes title of shogun. Tokugawa rule established

'The Tale of Genji' written by Murasaki Shikibu

School of Zen Buddhism founded

Noh theatre develops

Growth of Edo, Osaka and castle towns

Zen culture spreads

'Tales of Heike' and other stories about war become popular

Kabuki, Bunraku and other arts flourish

1185 Minamoto clan defeats Taira clan

1543 firearms introduced

1635 Japanese banned from travelling abroad

1853 US ships arrive. Japan opens its ports to foreigners

1639 All Europeans, except a few Dutch traders, asked to leave Japan

1467-77 Onin Wars

KAMAKURA (1185)   MUROMACHI AND MOMOYAMA (1392)   EDO (1600)   MEIJI (1868)

A land of contrasts

Japan is made up of around 3,900 islands which were once part of the Asian mainland. They broke off gradually during the last ice age, about 12,000 years ago. There is **archaeological** and **anthropological** evidence that mainland peoples from China and Korea, and Pacific Islanders from the south, continued to migrate to the islands of Japan over thousands of years.

THE FOUR MAIN ISLANDS OF JAPAN – Hokkaido, Honshu, Shikoku and Kyushu – are heavily forested, with lush, sometimes impassable mountains (many of them volcanic), fast-flowing rivers and fertile plains. Isolated families, or clans, grew up in remote, sheltered valleys. Their **Shinto** religion (see page 56) sprang from their respect for the forces of nature.

◁ *Japan's many islands stretch across 3,800 km, from the cool north to the semi-tropical islands of Okinawa in the south. Its neighbours are North and South Korea, China and Russia.*

△ *This map shows a few of the crops that are grown on Japan's four main islands, and the types of fish that are found in the coastal waters.*

WITH SO MANY MOUNTAINS AND FORESTS, Japan has little grazing land for animals. So most people rely on rice, fish and vegetables for food.

rice

seaweed

mulberry bush

tea

oranges

lemons

squid

crab

clam

octopus

salmon

tuna

Hokkaido

THE CLIMATE varies from cool summers and snowy winters in the north, to hot, humid summers and cool winters in the south.

EARTHQUAKES AND TYPHOONS are common. There can be 7,000 to 8,000 tremors every year, but most are hardly noticeable. Typhoons strike every year, badly damaging crops and houses.

▽ *Ainu women often tattooed their mouths with soot as a way of warding off evil spirits.*

Edo (Tokyo)

THE AINU PEOPLE of Hokkaido appear to have a different origin from the rest of the Japanese population. As well as looking very different, their beliefs and language are not the same. Some experts think the Ainu may have come to Japan from Siberia thousands of years ago, but no one is sure. Originally, they lived in Honshu, but were driven out and finally settled in Hokkaido. Very few Ainu remain today.

Layers of wealth and status

THE TYPES OF CLOTHES worn by Japanese people through history can tell us a lot about society at that time. For example, in the Heian period, nobles had the time and money to worry about the smallest detail of their clothing. Their clothes were designed to look impressive – often at the expense of comfort. For people who worked outdoors, such as farmers, clothes had to be practical, inexpensive and hard-wearing. By the Edo period, wealthy townspeople enjoyed dressing in the latest fashions. The **shogunate** authorities were worried by displays of wealth and made rules to make sure everyone dressed according to their class in **society**.

straw cloak

🐸 **CRAFTSMEN** were ranked below farmers, but above merchants, because they made things that were useful, such as samurai swords, or cooking pots.

headband

short kimono, or happi coat

straw sandals

farmer's wife

farmer in winter dress

craftsman

🐸 **FARMERS** were valued in society because they paid taxes to the **daimyo** in the form of rice and, occasionally, money. Some farmers owned land and were rich, but most were poor workers. Although clothes varied from region to region, farmers usually wore short jackets and trousers made from cotton or hemp. In hot weather, they just wore a loincloth – a strip of material that went around their hips and between their legs. One way women kept cool was by loosening their clothing a little.

🐸 **MERCHANTS** were generally despised by the authorities, because they did not actually make anything. Instead, they made money by buying and selling the work of others. However, during the Edo period, when the samurai lost their influence, some merchants grew increasingly wealthy and powerful. The authorities tried to stop the merchants from showing off their wealth, by telling them not to wear expensive silks. The merchants got around this rule by lining their cotton robes with silk.

samurai and wife

layers of silk kimono

wide sash, or obi

kimono (our version is raised at the front to display the shoes)

over-jacket, or kataginu, with family crest

simple, cotton kimono

wooden shoes, or geta

silk lining

toe socks, or tabi

🐸 **WIVES** of high ranking samurai put on layers of silk kimono, with the lighter colours worn underneath. Small, overall patterns were fashionable, as were padded hems that dragged along the floor.

🐸 **THE SAMURAI** were the highest class in society. They were the only people allowed to carry two swords. They had two types of dress: everyday and ceremonial, shown above.

merchant

THE BASIC JAPANESE garment for both men and women was a loose-fitting coat with a tie belt. It is called a kimono, a word which means 'the thing worn' and can be used to describe anything from a short smock to the most elaborate gown. Kimono probably originated in ancient China: styles and accessories varied through the centuries, according to fashion and the sex and marital status of the wearer. In general, ordinary people wore simple, practical clothes, increasing the layers according to the season. The ruling classes wore multi-layered, fashionable robes to reflect their status in society.

IN THE HEIAN PERIOD, people wore an undergarment called a *kosode*, a plain T-shaped wrap with short sleeves, with a pair of wide, baggy trousers called *hakama* underneath. Over the years, dress became simpler and eventually the *kosode* became the outer garment. Once outside, it became highly decorated instead of plain.

△ *Ivory or wooden toggles, called netsuke, were used to anchor small items kept in the waist sash of a kimono. This ivory netsuke is a carving of Hotei, the god of luck.*

MAKE A KIMONO

You will need: dark blue fabric, white fabric, needle and thread, glue, black paint, pins, chalk

1 To make the back panel, lie down on the dark blue fabric and ask a friend to draw a rectangle shape around you with the chalk. The rectangle should flare out slightly at the bottom, as shown above. Cut out the shape carefully.

2 Cut out two front panels as above. They should be the same length as the back panel and half its width. They should curve slightly at the top.

3 Lie the back of the kimono flat on the floor. Place the front panels on top, lining up the top and side edges. Sew front and back panels together along the top and down the sides. Leave a gap for the sleeves.

4 Cut out two large sleeve shapes as shown above left. Fold the sleeves in half so that the curved edges meet at the bottom. Sew up the bottom edge and along the curved edge. Leave a gap for your hand to go through.

5 Cut a strip of white material for the neckband, 13 cm wide and long enough to fit along the entire front edge of the kimono, as above.

△ *To make a girl's waist sash, or obi, paint a plain piece of material and wrap it around your kimono twice.*

KIMONO were carefully picked to match the season, or even a particular festival. A plain, elegant style, for example, might be worn for a ceremonial occasion. Artists of the Edo period made woodblock prints showing the latest kimono designs. Ordinary people bought prints to pick up hints on what was fashionable. Kimono could be worth a great deal money and were an important part of a woman's dowry when she got married.

NOBLEWOMEN wore many layers of beautiful silks. On top of their red *hakama*, they put on different-coloured robes with long sleeves. When they went out in their carriages, they left one sleeve dangling outside, so that everyone who saw them would admire their good taste. For court duties and weddings, between 15 and 40 robes were worn (the larger people looked, the richer they were thought to be). In the 12th century, the number of robes worn was reduced from 12 to five.

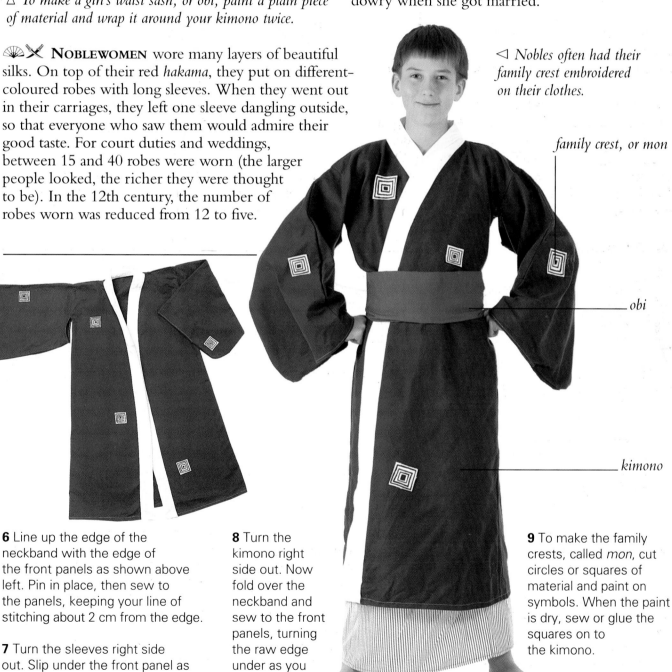

◁ *Nobles often had their family crest embroidered on their clothes.*

family crest, or mon

obi

kimono

6 Line up the edge of the neckband with the edge of the front panels as shown above left. Pin in place, then sew to the panels, keeping your line of stitching about 2 cm from the edge.

7 Turn the sleeves right side out. Slip under the front panel as shown above left, and sew in place, leaving a gap underneath the arm.

8 Turn the kimono right side out. Now fold over the neckband and sew to the front panels, turning the raw edge under as you go to make a hem.

9 To make the family crests, called *mon*, cut circles or squares of material and paint on symbols. When the paint is dry, sew or glue the squares on to the kimono.

MAKE-UP was another way of showing how important people were. Wealthy men and women whitened their faces because it distinguished them from tanned and weatherbeaten workers, and because a pale face was considered very beautiful. Small cotton bags filled with rice powder were moistened with perfumed water and dabbed over their faces. White lead was also used and there were many cases of people being poisoned because lead is highly toxic.

THE TYPE OF HAT, or *kammuri*, a man wore was one way to tell what rank he held. The *kammuri* was made of a silk fabric that was **lacquered** and made to look stiff. High-ranking nobles wore dark or pale violet *kammuri*, while less important nobles wore black (see page 23).

WOMEN'S HAIR was considered beautiful if it was long, thick and shining – like the wing of a raven. If a woman's hair did not match this ideal, then she might wear a wig. In the Heian and Kamakura periods, women kept their hair loose, but in other eras it was fashionable to pin it up.

△ *Samurai warriors shaved the tops of their heads, then gathered the hair at the sides and back into a ponytail, which they doubled over and tied tightly.*

MEN'S HAIRSTYLES were another mark of rank. Ordinary workers wore their hair short, while noblemen wore their hair in a topknot. Up until the Edo period, nobles grew moustaches and beards, but samurai kept their faces free of hair. Monks plucked their faces and shaved their heads.

MAKE A PAIR OF JAPANESE SHOES (GETA)

You will need: two pieces of wood, 1.5 cm thick, four blocks of wood, 1.5 cm thick, string, masking tape, calico, shiny material, paint, strong nails, hammer, glue, hand drill, saw

1 Ask an adult to help cut the wooden base of the shoes, slightly longer and wider than your foot. Cut the corners so they are rounded. For the struts, cut four blocks of wood 5 cm deep and as wide as the base.

2 Drill three holes in each base, as shown. Nail two struts to each base, one 4 cm from the top, the other 4 cm from the bottom. Paint the shoes brown.

3 Cut two rectangles of shiny material as long as the shoe and 10 cm wide. Then cut two smaller rectangles of calico. Put the calico on the shiny material and place a length of string in the middle, as shown.

4 Now, roll up the material and the string to make two padded tubes, or thongs. Glue the edges down. Glue thin strips of material around the string at the ends of each thong.

5 Pass a string loop through the hole in the front of the shoe. Thread the thong through and knot the loop. Pass the ends of the thong through the remaining holes, knot underneath and secure with masking tape.

SAMURAI WARRIORS kept their hair neat and tightly tied. It could be very embarrassing if a samurai's hair came undone in battle and it was considered a terrible disgrace if an opponent lopped off his ponytail.

If a samurai was feeling ill, he would not bother to shave his head. His hair might grow into a messy tangle, but he would be careful never to be seen in public looking like this.

▷ *Apart from haircombs and netsuke, Japanese women did not wear jewellery. Haircombs and pins were made of ivory, horn, wood or metal and often painted.*

WOMEN reddened their lips with a spot of crushed flower-petal paste on the lower lip to make their mouths look smaller. They also plucked their eyebrows and painted black marks high on their foreheads with a paste of soot and glue. Natural eyebrows were thought to be vulgar, like 'fat caterpillars' crawling on the face.

△ *Some hairstyles were very elaborate. To keep them in place, both men and women slept with their heads on padded, wooden headrests instead of pillows.*

TEETH BLACKENING was commonly practised by the upper classes, a custom that spread to the other classes over the centuries. As the Japanese had very little calcium in their diet (no milk or cheese), adult teeth were often naturally blackened with decay. Black teeth, therefore, became a sign of maturity, and white teeth were thought to look as 'naked as a skinned animal'. Married women were the only people who did not blacken their teeth.

△ *Geta were useful for keeping the wearer's feet dry in rainy weather. Today, they are sometimes worn with traditional costume.*

FOOTWEAR for ordinary people was a pair of thong sandals made of straw. When it rained, they wore *geta,* simple wooden clogs that kept their feet clear of the mud. Hunters and warriors wore shoes made of leather, and wealthy people wore lacquered wooden *geta* with high platforms and comfortably padded insides. **Geisha** were women who worked in the entertainment business. They wore *geta* so high they could not walk without the help of their servants. Sometimes two-toed, padded cotton socks, called *tabi,* were worn. The thong of the *geta* was slipped between the big toe and second toe.

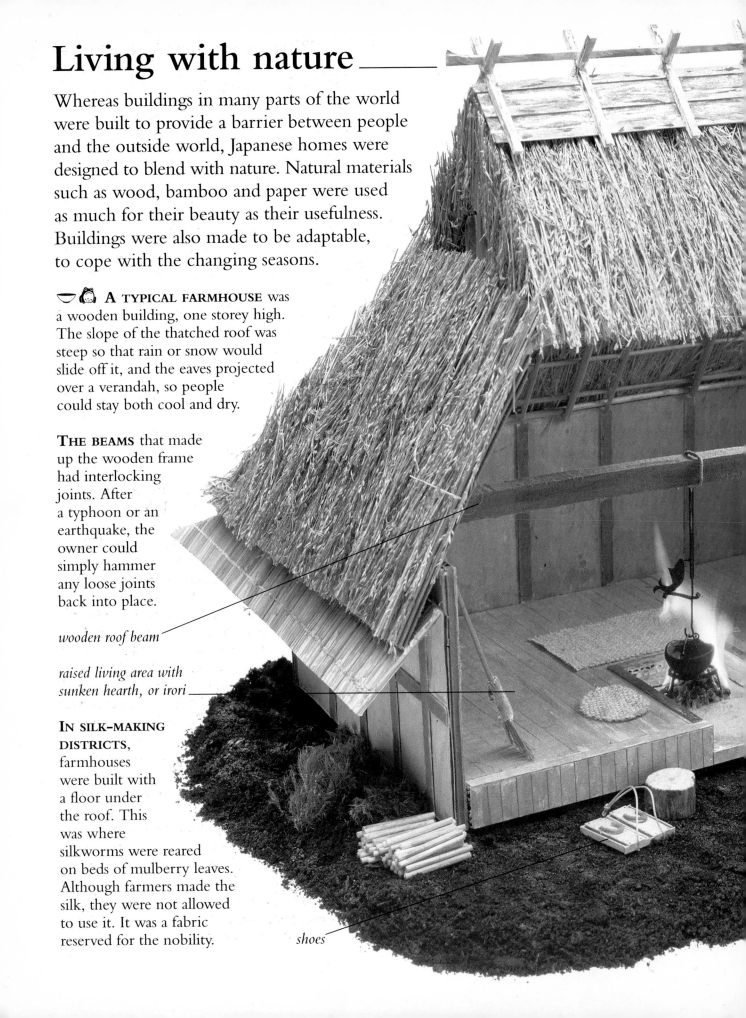

Living with nature

Whereas buildings in many parts of the world
were built to provide a barrier between people
and the outside world, Japanese homes were
designed to blend with nature. Natural materials
such as wood, bamboo and paper were used
as much for their beauty as their usefulness.
Buildings were also made to be adaptable,
to cope with the changing seasons.

A TYPICAL FARMHOUSE was
a wooden building, one storey high.
The slope of the thatched roof was
steep so that rain or snow would
slide off it, and the eaves projected
over a verandah, so people
could stay both cool and dry.

THE BEAMS that made
up the wooden frame
had interlocking
joints. After
a typhoon or an
earthquake, the
owner could
simply hammer
any loose joints
back into place.

wooden roof beam

*raised living area with
sunken hearth, or irori*

**IN SILK-MAKING
DISTRICTS,**
farmhouses
were built with
a floor under
the roof. This
was where
silkworms were reared
on beds of mulberry leaves.
Although farmers made the
silk, they were not allowed
to use it. It was a fabric
reserved for the nobility.

shoes

thatched straw roof

wooden ladder for roof repairs

△ *The kitchen was usually situated at ground level. It was full of utensils for cleaning, chopping and cooking food.*

BEFORE MOVING IN to their new house, a family fixed charms to the roof to frighten away demons. Then, a sign with the owner's name on it was hung above the door to show that the family had moved in.

ALL THE VILLAGERS helped each other to build and repair their houses, under the guidance of the village carpenter. The main pillars were set in place one **ken** apart (about the length of a man lying down) followed by the roof beams. The floorboards were laid on a raised framework, then the sunken hearth, or *irori*, was built. Once the roof was thatched and the outer walls filled in, the house was finished. The villagers then held a celebratory feast with the carpenter as guest of honour.

INTERIORS were very simple. Cleanliness was a priority for Japanese people, so outdoor shoes were always removed before stepping on to the raised wooden platform that was the living, eating and sleeping area. A bucket or tub was conveniently placed at the entrance to wash muddy feet. Clean water for preparing and cooking food was kept in a wooden trough at the back of the house.

bucket for carrying fresh water

frame for carrying loads

JAPANESE HOMES were designed to adapt to the seasons. In winter, blinds were kept shut and screens, paper walls and wooden shutters helped to keep the cold out. In summer, these things were swept aside to allow in cooling breezes.

TOWN HOUSES for the merchant class were built close together in rows along the streets, with small gardens at the rear. The houses had similar features to the farmhouses, such as small rooms separated by sliding doors.

ROOMS could be used for several purposes. Screens and sliding paper walls could easily be moved and put somewhere else. If a family was holding a party, for example, the paper walls could be taken out to make the room larger.

SCREENS were used to block drafts and for privacy. Most people used screens made of wicker, but in a wealthy home there might be several decorated screens of lacquered bamboo, sometimes framed with gold and encrusted with gems.

MAKE A PAPER SCREEN

You will need: 24 cardboard strips, 60 cm x 1.5 cm, 12 cardboard strips, 40 cm x 1.5 cm, masking tape, black paint, string, glue, scissors, white tissue paper 61 cm x 41 cm.

1 Tape each long strip to another strip of the same length to make 12 extra-thick strips. The screen is made of three panels. To make one panel, tape four short strips horizontally to four long vertical strips, as shown above.

2 Paint the panel black. When the paint is dry, spread glue on one side of the panel and lay the tissue paper over it, keeping it flat and smooth. When the glue is dry, trim the excess paper.

3 Make another two panels in this way. To join the panels, make a hole through the frame and paper at the top and bottom of the screens. Thread string through and tie the panels together, as shown below. Keep the strings loose, so the panels can be folded.

▽ *Interior of a late-Edo town house.*

hanging scroll ____

alcove, or tokonoma ____

tatami

THE BEST ROOM IN THE HOUSE had an alcove with a raised floor, called a *tokonoma*. This was used to display a piece of pottery or a flower arrangement. On the wall hung a picture, or some calligraphy. Originally, a *tokonoma* was reserved for the samurai class, but by the Edo period, most people had one in their home.

TATAMI are straw and rush mats made to standard sizes of one *ken* long and half a *ken* wide. Two *tatami* side by side form a square. This was then used to calculate the size of rooms.

COOKING EQUIPMENT included oil jars, cauldrons, trays, buckets, bowls, baskets and boxes, as well as cleavers, a variety of sharp knives, mortars and pestles. It was all stowed away neatly in wooden chests.

wooden chest of drawers

paper lantern

paper windows, or shoji

low eating table *paper screen* *raised wooden hearth*

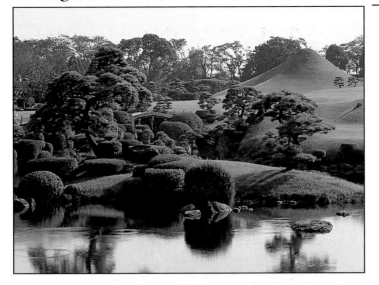

⬯ **THE WALLS** that surrounded the castle and formed the foundations of the keep were built of stones carefully piled on top of each other. The base of the walls curved outwards for stability, then rose smoothly and vertically, which made them very difficult to climb. Defence ditches and moats meant that the only way in to the castle was over a series of portable bridges, which could be removed in case of attack.

▽ *Castles were usually built on raised ground, so the shogun could protect the surrounding rice paddies that were the source of his wealth.*

△ *Within the castle walls, the daimyo created peaceful gardens where he could contemplate the beauty of nature.*

⬯ **IN THE 16TH CENTURY,** guns and cannons were introduced to Japan. The flimsy, wooden military fortresses built by the shogun and samurai to keep order in the land, became vulnerable. The shogun had to build permanent castle compounds, with strong stone walls to withstand gunshot and cannonballs.

small keep

windows for throwing stones or boiling water on to the enemy

gaps for firing guns and arrows

gateway to inner courtyard

⬯ **TOWNS GREW UP** around the castle walls and the merchants who supplied the castle and the samurai moved there with their families. These settlements became known as 'below the castle towns', and they formed the basis for many of the major towns in modern Japan.

◯ **NEAR THE SHOGUN'S QUARTERS** there were further defence systems. Guards hid in secret chambers, ready to leap out and attack intruders. The floor of the corridor leading to the shogun's rooms was specially made with planks that squeaked. It was known as a 'nightingale' corridor because it 'sang' if someone tried to creep silently along it.

◯ **AT THE HEART** of every castle compound was the keep, or *tenshu*. The main keep was usually made up of seven interlinking storeys. The doors and screens of the rooms within were decorated by the best artists in the land.

garden with
fish pool

castle keep

plastered timber walls

ceramic tiled roof

raised stone walls

moat

Life at court

In 794, the Emperor Kammu moved his court to a place he called Heian-kyo, meaning 'capital of peace and tranquillity' (now Kyoto). For four centuries court life flourished there. In the early part of this period, courtiers copied the ways of their sophisticated neighbours, the Chinese, but by 1,000, a distinctly Japanese culture began to appear.

STYLE AND MANNERS were very important in the Heian court. Noblewomen for instance, wore at least 12 different coloured silk robes, and spent many hours choosing the colours and deciding in which order to wear them. Getting dressed was a form of art. Paintings from this time often show women elegantly collapsed in a billow of clothing, most likely staggering under the weight of their garments.

MAKE A FAN

2 Lie the strips on top of one another and pull the thread through the holes at the bottom. Secure the bundle of strips by tying on one button at the front and another at the back.

3 Spread the fan out and sew thread through the holes in the top, as shown above left. Knot the thread at each end. Now paint a cherry tree on the open fan.

You will need: cream card, paints, paintbrush, two buttons, needle, drawing compass, coloured threads

1 Carefully cut the cream card into 16 tapering strips, 24 cm long x 3.5 cm wide at the top. Round off the top of each strip, and trim the bottom. Use the compass to make a hole in the centre of each strip at the top and bottom, as above.

4 Add pale pink blossom to the branches of your tree design. When the paint is dry, decorate the fan with long lengths of plaited threads tied to the sides.

THE MAIN DISTRACTIONS at court were love affairs and religious occasions. Courtiers dressed in colourful costumes and sang and danced at religious ceremonies. Trips to the countryside became an important event in their lives. Courtiers would travel to see flowers in bloom, or to enjoy the smells of different incense woods.

△ *It was the custom for noblewomen to hide their faces from men, so they used beautifully decorated fans as screens.*

ARISTOCRATIC FAMILIES lived in mansions consisting of a main hall connected to various pavilions by galleries. Their houses were set in landscaped gardens with lakes and little islands, enclosed by walls. The pavilions were, like the homes of most people, simply furnished and icy cold in winter. Mealtimes were simple affairs, too. Dishes of rice, seaweed, fruit and vegetables were enjoyed at the two main meals of the day, which were taken at about 10 am and 4 pm.

LITERARY AND CALLIGRAPHY SKILLS were held in high regard by both sexes. Most nobles wrote poetry, which was especially important for conducting love affairs. Women of the period were known for their elegant novels, diaries, love letters and poetry. In fact, Japan's earliest and most famous novel, an epic of 1,000 pages called '*The Tale of Genji*', was written by a Heian lady of the court called Murasaki Shikibu. It tells of the life and many loves of a prince.

MARRIAGES between noblemen and women were arranged for the benefit of their families. It was common practice for a wife and her children to remain at home with her family, and be visited there by her husband.

▷ *This nobleman and woman show their high rank by wearing costly silks. The man also wears a kammuri, a hat reserved for court members.*

Daily life in the town

The city of Edo was for many years the largest, most sophisticated city in the world. It was a centre for trade and all of Japan's main highways met there. The *daimyo* all had large houses in Edo, and there were temples, theatres and shops of every kind. Not surprisingly, life in Edo was quite different from life in a village.

CHILDREN were prepared for their future lives at home. Girls learned how to sew, cook and wash, while boys learned their father's trade, or were sent off to learn the trade of one of his friends. In the spring and summer, children played games outside, or went hunting for crickets and fireflies. During the winter months, families spent their evenings together, reading, talking or playing board games such as **Go**, a game that is still popular in Japan today.

△ *A bathhouse was the perfect place for townspeople to relax. The one above is fed by hot spring water.*

BOYS AND GIRLS were taught to read, write and do arithmetic in schools, which were often attached to temples. Sons of military families were often sent away to be taught by monks, or to the homes of even richer families where they were educated in return for their services as **pages**. Merchants made sure their daughters were educated too, so they could help to run the family business.

▷ *At New Year, children played with spinning tops made of bamboo and paper.*

MEN were the providers, although women were usually in charge of the family finances. Men were sometimes accused by their wives of wasting the family's money in the town's theatres, restaurants and bars. However, as heads of the household, men felt they had the freedom to behave as they pleased, whatever their wives said.

WOMEN were expected to do all the housework and cooking, with the help of servants if the family could afford them. Wives served their husbands at mealtimes, but did not eat with them. Among the merchant class, some women owned property and ran businesses and shops. Women were usually very busy with household duties, but occasionally they went on pilgrimages, or visited the theatre. Many women looked forward to the day when they would have a daughter-in-law to take over the housework.

MOST TOWN HOUSES did not have baths, so public baths were very popular. These were places where men and women could relax and gossip, as well as get clean. As soap was expensive, people used rice bran to wash with instead.

1 Ask an adult to help you cut out four pieces of balsa wood in the shape shown left. They should be 37 cm long x 13 cm wide at the top.

2 Glue two shapes together to make one bat. Repeat for the other bat. Copy or trace your chosen design onto the bats, as shown above.

3 Paint the handle and the middle section to look like wood. Then colour in your design and the stripes. Finally, paint the shuttlecock gold, red and orange.

You will need: four pieces of balsa wood, pencil, paintbrush and paints, a shuttlecock, craft knife

△ *Originally, battledore was played with a soya bean instead of a shuttlecock. Beans were believed to ward off evil and disease.*

CHILDREN looked forward to several events throughout the year. Perhaps the most enjoyable was New Year, when many games were played. Battledore, or shuttlecock, was a popular New Year's present for girls. Like badminton, the game is played with two people who try to keep the shuttlecock in the air for as long as possible.

The warrior class

Towards the end of the Heian period, many wars raged throughout Japan. This led to the rise of a group of warrior noblemen called *bushi* ('fighting men'), or samurai. The samurai had an important influence on Japanese society, up until the 19th century.

▷ *This 17th century samurai dolphin helmet is made from leather, lacquer and gilt. It was meant to make a samurai look impressive, so that he could frighten the enemy.*

⚔ **A WARRIOR GOVERNMENT** seized power from the emperor in the 12th century. Although the emperor and his court continued to live in the capital Kyoto, real power was held by the military ruler, known as the shogun, in the city of Kamakura. The shogun was served by a loyal band of samurai.

⚔ MAKE A SAMURAI SWORD

You will need: cardboard, paper, glue gold paint, black and white cotton strips

1 Cut a curved sword shape 5 cm wide x 75 cm long from cardboard, as above.

2 Cut a round guard 7.5 cm in diameter with a slit in the centre. Slide the guard over the sword as above. Wrap strips of cotton around the sword and glue in place.

3 Paint the sword gold. For the grip, cut two pieces of card and glue as shown. Wrap with black cotton. Finally, decorate your sword.

🐸 **THE SAMURAI** were fearless fighters who trained for years to learn the skills of swordsmanship and archery. The training was very demanding: as well as learning how to fight, the samurai had to go for long periods without food to test their endurance. They were also taught to think and behave in a special way called the *bushido*, or 'way of the warrior'. By learning the *bushido*, a samurai warrior had an almost religious devotion to carrying out his duties. He was also prepared to die for the shogun, if necessary.

THE SWORD was the samurai's most valuable possession and was handed down from father to son. Those who made swords were highly respected, and even dressed in the white robes of a Shinto priest. Sword blades were made of a combination of hard and soft metal, and were so sharp that they could behead an enemy with a single blow. Sword guards, or *tsuba*, were beautifully decorated to reflect the skill needed to make the blade.

▷ The samurai wore light and loose-fitting clothes, so they could move quickly in battle. Armour was worn over the top for protection.

helmet with horns to frighten the enemy

neck shields

SAMURAI ARMOUR was made of hundreds of scales made from lacquered iron. These scales were tied together in rows with silk cord. The way they were linked together made the armour very strong, giving the samurai the protection they needed.

△ This 19th-century Japanese sword guard shows three holy men, **Confucius**, **Buddha** and Lao-Tse, tasting rice wine beneath a pine tree.

breastplate

WHEN FACING THE ENEMY, the samurai performed a number of rituals. Each warrior announced his name, family background and a list of brave deeds he had done. Then the battle would begin. The victor praised his enemy before cutting off his head. In case his life should end in the same way, a samurai always burned incense in his helmet, so that if his head was cut off in battle, it would still smell sweet!

sword hangs from the waist

iron-scale armour

FOR HUNDREDS OF YEARS the samurai were valued for their skill at warfare. During the Edo period, peace spread throughout Japan. After this, the samurai became more involved with administrative duties and matters of ceremony than with fighting.

boots made of leather, or bearskin with studded soles

Seasons and celebrations

Life, for the Japanese, strictly followed the rhythms of nature. Different foods were eaten according to the season and homes were rearranged to cope with the changing weather. Even the Japanese calendar of celebrations and festivals was based on ancient ceremonies to mark the yearly planting, growing and harvesting cycles.

MAKE A CARP STREAMER

You will need:
thin paper, paintbrush, paint, masking tape, glue, scissors, string, length of thin, flexible cane

1 Lie two sheets of thin paper on top of each other, draw a fish shape, including fins and tail, as above.

2 Cut out the shape and paint the fish on one side of each piece of paper. Gluing the edges only, stick the two plain sides of the fish together. Leave the mouth and tail unglued.

3 Tape the cane into a circle and place it inside the fish's mouth. Fold the fish's lips over it and tape in place. Tie string to the hoop to hang or fly your carp.

△ *During the Doll Festival, girls have parties for their friends and have special sweets and drinks.*

SPRING begins in early February when the plum trees bloom, and ends with Boys' Day (now Childrens' Day) on 5 May.

▷ *Families with sons still hang carp streamers from poles outside their homes on Boys' Day.*

BOYS' DAY was originally a festival to prepare farm labourers for the hard work of transplanting rice seedlings. In Heian times it was known as the sweet flag festival (named after a type of plant) and people hung out stems of sweet flag to keep evil away from their homes. As the stem of sweet flag looks like a sword, the ceremony gradually became a celebration of martial arts. By the Edo period, the festival was associated with symbols of manliness and courage. The paper carp that hang from flagpoles today on Boys' Day are symbols of courage and ambition, in recognition of an age-old tale of a carp which once swam all the way to heaven to become a dragon. Displays of dolls are also common today, with models of folk heroes, warriors and emperors.

THE DOLL FESTIVAL was celebrated on 3 March in households where there were daughters. In Edo times, a whole room was used to display dolls, usually the emperor and empress in Heian costume. As well as celebrating daughters, the festival was supposed to ward off evil spirits.

REFRESHING FOODS, such as cold soups, noodles and **tofu**, were served on white or glass plates in summer. Juicy fruits were also popular.

ROOMS WERE KEPT COOL by hanging bamboo or cloth blinds that allowed cooling breezes in, but kept out the glare of the summer sun.

▽ *Candlelit lanterns were used in summer to cast moving shadows on the walls. This gave the effect of being in a cool, shady forest.*

SUMMER starts in early May, when misty rains fall for about four weeks. Crops grow thick and fast, and it is very humid. In July, the heat is almost unbearable. Gifts of cooling foods, such as water-melon, are sent with greetings to mark the end of summer on 7 August. *Obon* is the main holiday of the season, based on an ancient custom of welcoming the souls of ancestors.

THE MOON FESTIVAL was celebrated in August. In the Heian period, parties of people went out at night to view the moon and write poems praising its beauty. Music was played gently in the background to add to the atmosphere and make the occasion more special.

AUTUMN was seen as a welcome release from the heat of summer. The Japanese went on special trips to see the most colourful displays of autumn leaves. The fading beauty of autumn has also inspired much Japanese poetry and painting.

◁ *This fan represents the full moon and is decorated with autumn flowers and leaves.*

MAKE A KITE

You will need:
lengths of flexible cane: 2 x 80 cm long, 1 x 96 cm long, string, paint, masking tape, glue, thin paper, scissors, dowelling, or bamboo

1 To make the kite frame, tape the ends of the shorter lengths of cane together to make a large loop as shown right. Then cross the ends of the long piece of cane and tape them together as above.

2 Tape the crossed length of cane on top of the loop. Place the cane frame on the paper and trace around the shape, drawing a square to cover the crossed cane at the bottom. Allow an extra 2 cm all around to fold over the frame.

3 Draw and paint your design on the paper as shown above. (You can use the large image on the right as your guide.) Leave to dry thoroughly.

4 Cut out the design and place on the frame. Trim the edges and glue in place. Now tie two pieces of string from the top to the bottom of each wing. Stretch a piece of string across the wings, to curve the kite.

5 Cut three pieces of string, 60 cm long. Tie one to the top of each wing, and the third to the centre of the body. Tie the loose ends to a long string, wound onto a piece of dowel or bamboo.

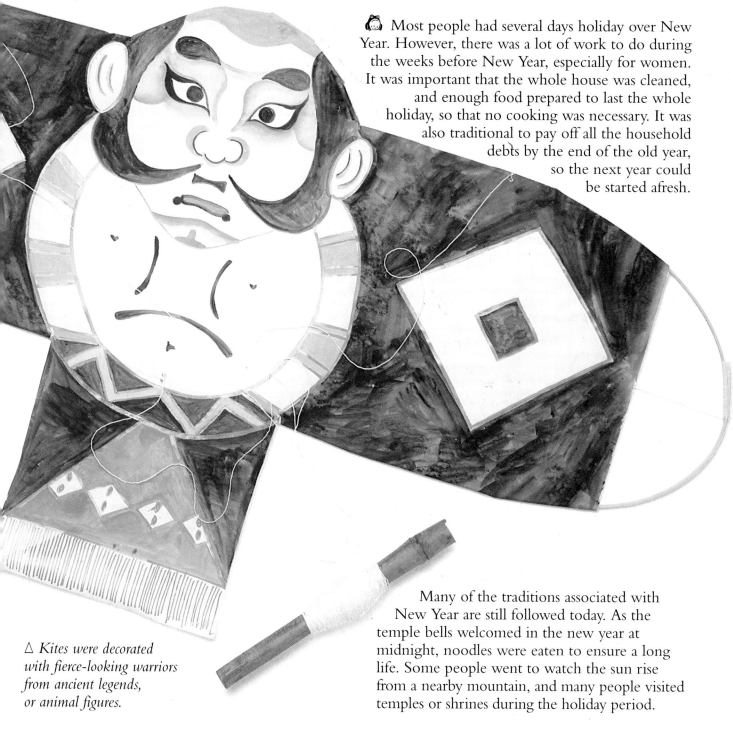

🐸 Most people had several days holiday over New Year. However, there was a lot of work to do during the weeks before New Year, especially for women. It was important that the whole house was cleaned, and enough food prepared to last the whole holiday, so that no cooking was necessary. It was also traditional to pay off all the household debts by the end of the old year, so the next year could be started afresh.

△ Kites were decorated with fierce-looking warriors from ancient legends, or animal figures.

NEW YEAR was, and still is, the biggest festival of the Japanese year. Lots of games are played at this time, and in the Edo period, making and flying paper kites was very popular. As well as being fun, kite-flying had a religious significance. The kite was seen as a link between heaven and earth, so that when a kite was sent up into the sky, the Japanese believed they were sending a prayer up to the gods.

Many of the traditions associated with New Year are still followed today. As the temple bells welcomed in the new year at midnight, noodles were eaten to ensure a long life. Some people went to watch the sun rise from a nearby mountain, and many people visited temples or shrines during the holiday period.

Different types of food were eaten during New Year. Home-made rice cakes called *mochi* were very popular. Each member of the family took turns pounding the cakes into the right shape and texture. They also offered the cakes to the gods of the household and to their ancestors by placing several cakes on the Buddhist and Shinto altars in the house.

Rice, fish and vegetables

Japan is a country of steep mountains, which makes growing crops very difficult. It also means that there is only a small amount of land available for farming. Despite the problems, rice was introduced in the first century and has remained the staple food of the Japanese ever since.

PLANTING, GROWING AND HARVESTING RICE was hard, time-consuming work. All the people in a village gathered together to help plant and harvest this vital crop.

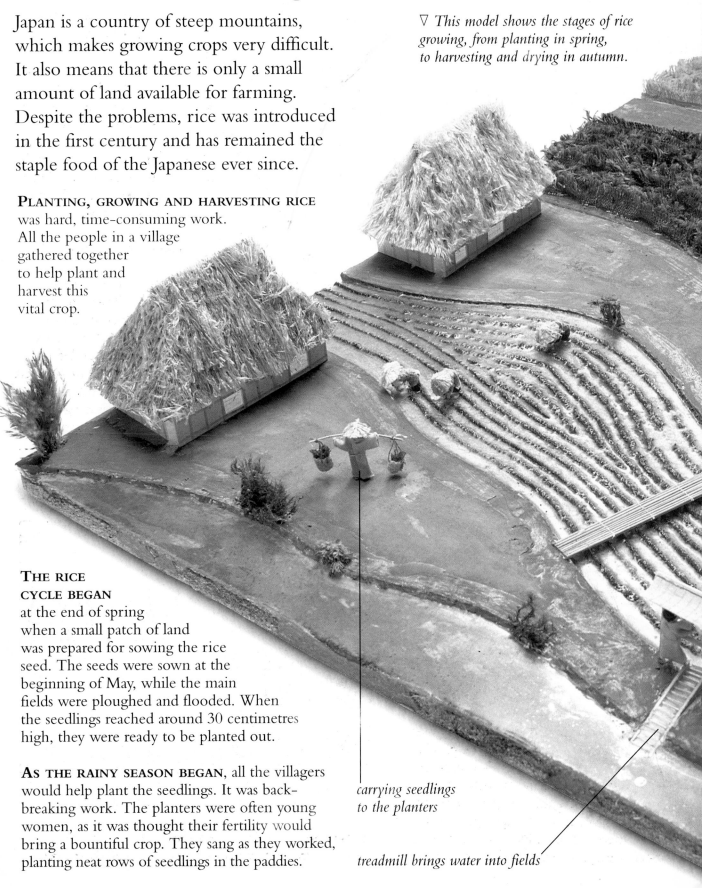

▽ *This model shows the stages of rice growing, from planting in spring, to harvesting and drying in autumn.*

THE RICE CYCLE BEGAN at the end of spring when a small patch of land was prepared for sowing the rice seed. The seeds were sown at the beginning of May, while the main fields were ploughed and flooded. When the seedlings reached around 30 centimetres high, they were ready to be planted out.

AS THE RAINY SEASON BEGAN, all the villagers would help plant the seedlings. It was back-breaking work. The planters were often young women, as it was thought their fertility would bring a bountiful crop. They sang as they worked, planting neat rows of seedlings in the paddies.

carrying seedlings to the planters

treadmill brings water into fields

stripping, or heckling, the harvested rice

AS THE PLANTS GREW, they had to be kept clear of weeds and the water level checked constantly. If water was scarce, the farmers might argue over their share, and some would even divert water away from a neighbour's field and into their own.

harvesting the rice using sickles

HARVESTING took place around October or November. The water was allowed to drain away from the field and then sickles were used to harvest the rice. The long sheaves of rice were gathered into bundles, or circular stacks and left to dry in the sun. Then the grain was stripped, or heckled, by pulling the plant between two sticks, or hitting the plant against a large, open barrel. The remaining grain was winnowed, or separated, by being thrown up into the air. The farmer was left with brown, unpolished rice still covered in its outer husk. Once the harvest was complete, the tax collector visited each farm to calculate the share of the rice to be paid to the *daimyo*.

young rice plants

raised bank or dyke separates the paddy fields

rice seedlings planted in flooded paddy field

🐸 **DIFFERENT METHODS** were used to keep the precious rice crop healthy. Some, such as spraying the fields with a mixture of whale oil and vinegar, were quite effective against hungry pests. Other methods included magic rituals, or offering prayers to the gods to bring rain.

△ *This farmer is using a water wheel. As he treads the wheel, water is scooped up and transferred into the rice field.*

JAPAN IS SURROUNDED BY SEA and has many lakes and rivers, so fish has always been an important part of the Japanese diet, providing much-needed protein. Popular varieties were sea bream, trout and salmon, and these were usually eaten raw. Other seafoods, such as octopus, shellfish and even fish eggs and eyes, were also collected and eaten. Oysters and some seaweed, such as *nori*, were known to have been farmed by the Japanese as long as 300 years ago.

FISHERMEN worked either part-time or full-time. Those who worked part-time spent most of the year farming, and only fished during the season. Full-time fisherman spent every day, weather permitting, going out to sea or along the rivers, and mending their nets and boats. Their wives would often help to support the family by growing some rice and vegetables.

LARGE FLEETS OF FISHING VESSELS set sail from the coasts around Edo. They were financed by the merchants and brought back daily catches that were sold as soon as they were unloaded. Ordinary people often fished in local lakes and rivers to supplement their basic diet.

▽ *Women gathered different types of seaweed and shellfish from the seashore to eat or sell at the market.*

mooring pole

△ *Cormorant fishermen suspended small fires in buckets from the bows of their boats to attract fish.*

ON SOME RIVERS, cormorants were trained to dive in the water and snap up the fish. A metal or rope ring around the birds' necks stopped them from swallowing, so the fishermen could retrieve the catch from their mouths.

thwart

bow

straw matting used for grip

scoop net

△ *On this boat, the fishing net was attached to the boat and carefully lowered into the water. After a while, the fishermen raised the net and scooped out any fish caught in the net.*

net

bamboo pole to support net

stern

steering oar

rudder

straw basket to store fish

THERE WERE MANY RITUALS attached to eating and drinking in Japan. Much care was taken with the preparation of food and drink. A lot of time and imagination went into making food look as attractive as possible, by choosing different colours and textures of food, and designing the food on beautiful plates and in small bowls.

FISH, rather than meat, was the main source of protein for most people. It could be eaten in many different ways: boiled, grilled, or cut into thin slices and dipped in **soy sauce** and eaten raw. Another popular dish was *sushi*: raw fish or vegetables rolled in **vinegared rice** and wrapped in seaweed.

TEA ARRIVED from China in the ninth century. At first it was used as a medicine, but by the 14th century, nobles and samurai drank it at social gatherings. It was not until a century later that tea became a popular drink for everyone. Then, it was sipped at the end of a meal to wash down the last few grains of rice.

DRINKING RICE WINE, or *sake*, was enjoyed by men and women, and there were several customs associated with drinking it. *Sake* was served only during the first part of the meal. It was considered very rude to pour your own, so people took turns to pour *sake* for one another.

MAKE SUSHI

You will need: vinegared rice, tofu, chopped, cooked mushrooms, crab sticks, cucumber, avocado, smoked salmon, a sheet of seaweed (*nori*) or steamed cabbage leaves, soy sauce, thin cane table mat

1 Place the seaweed on the mat. Cover the seaweed with rice, apart from one edge. Lie the fish and vegetables in strips across the rice.

2 Use the mat to roll the seaweed into a tube. The rice should be wrapped around the ingredients, like a swiss roll.

3 Unroll the mat. Slice the seaweed roll into pieces 4 cm across. Now, dip your sushi into the soy sauce and eat it.

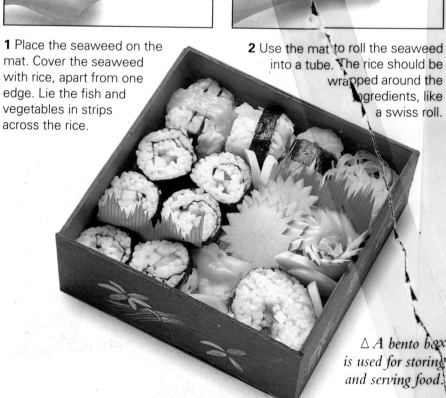

△ *A bento box is used for storing and serving food.*

CHOPSTICKS, or *hashi*, have been used in Japan for over a thousand years. They were usually made of wood, but they could also be made of ivory, bone, silver or gold. Extra long chopsticks were used for cooking and serving food. In Japan, chopsticks are pointed at one end, but in China they are blunt.

1 Hold the first chopstick between your thumb and first finger. Rest it lightly against your middle and third finger.

2 Hold the second chopstick between your thumb and first finger, resting it against your first and middle fingers.

3 Try to keep the first chopstick still and move the second chopstick up and down, so that the pointed ends touch each other.

◁ *The type of hand-rolled sushi shown here was first eaten towards the end of the Edo period. But raw fish, dipped in soy sauce, called sashimi, dates back even further.*

Getting around

Travelling in Japan before the Edo period was difficult. Steep mountains and rivers, and heavy rains and typhoons made travelling hazardous. A few determined people travelled on official business, or made pilgrimages to holy shrines. It was not until the Edo period, when highways provided safer and more convenient links between towns and cities, that travel became easier for more people.

⁂ **DURING THE HEIAN PERIOD**, there were very few proper roads, and bands of robbers made them unsafe to use. However, nobles from the capital still ventured out on trips, either to see the cherry blossom, or to visit a local shrine.

△ *The palanquin was a type of bamboo box suspended from two poles. It was supported by men who were paid to carry passengers.*

⁂ **THE MAIN FORMS OF TRANSPORT** were the palanquin and the slow and uncomfortable ox-drawn carriage. Among the nobility, carriages were a status symbol. Nobles competed with one another by showing off their beautiful carriages, although there were many rules about the kind of carriages that low or high ranking nobles could travel in. The imperial family travelled in the most elaborate of all. Their carriage had a green gabled roof and was so high that a ladder was needed to climb into the seat.

▷ *This type of carriage was used mainly by the nobility at the time of the Heian court.*

△ *Due to the rough conditions of the highways, and the many mountains and rivers, most people travelled on foot.*

⁂ **TRAVEL BECAME EASIER** during the Edo period as more roads were built connecting major centres. Ordinary people travelled for business as well as pleasure. Nevertheless, people could not travel wherever and whenever they wanted. They needed special papers from the authorities which were checked by officials at certain intervals on the main routes.

THE TOKAIDO, or eastern sea road, was one of the most important highways at this time. It stretched from the city of Edo to Kyoto, providing a vital communication link between the cities. Messengers ran along the highway in relay teams, carrying important letters, or money from one city to another. Those running on business for the authorities carried lanterns marked 'official business' and were given special treatment at checkpoints and ferries.

PROCESSIONS OF DAIMYO and their servants frequently travelled from their estates to the capital, Edo. As the processions passed along the highways, ordinary people had to show their respect by moving to the side of the road and dropping to their knees. Post-stations were placed at regular intervals along the highway where the nobles could hire horses and porters.

carriage coated with black lacquer

small window

family crest

slatted screen entrance cover

oxen used to pull carriage

Transport and trade

With the growth of towns and large cities like Edo, and Osaka to the south-west, trade flourished. Improved methods of transport by road and sea meant that merchants were able to move their goods more easily around the country. Despite the authorities' attempts to stop the growing power of the merchant class, many merchants became very wealthy.

△ *Ferry boats were used to carry travellers across rivers. If there were no ferry boats, a porter would wade across the river, carrying the traveller and his belongings for a small fee.*

🐸 **TRADE BY ROAD AND SEA** increased throughout Japan. Waterways in particular were very important in the city of Edo. A system of canals was used, not only to move people from place to place, but also to move goods by barges from warehouses to different parts of the city. As the city grew larger, more bridges were built. The most famous bridge was called Nihonbashi.

△ *This is a screen painting of Nihonbashi, 'the bridge of Japan', the place where the five main highways of Japan met.*

🐸 **DURING THE EDO PERIOD,** trade with the outside world was very restricted. Japanese ships did not sail to other countries, and in 1635 the Japanese were forbidden to go abroad. A few Chinese and Dutch traders were allowed to live on a small island off Kyushu. As these were the only foreigners allowed to live inside Japan, the Japanese were naturally very curious about them. The Dutch traders were known as 'red hairs' because of their light coloured hair. Some Japanese people even thought that they had hoofs instead of feet.

SMALL JUNKS OR COASTAL SHIPS transported goods around the country, moving cargoes from harbour to harbour. One of the most important trade routes was between the cities of Osaka and Edo; large cargoes of rice, *sake* and soy sauce were ferried backwards and forwards.

bamboo poles crisscrossed over cargo

large sail made of hemp

◁ *The oban was a large, gold coin that was used mainly by samurai or wealthy merchants, or at special ceremonies.*

🐸 **MERCHANTS** grew increasingly important as Edo and Osaka became much more commercial. As well as opening shops in the cities, merchants acted as money-lenders to the samurai and made profits on the loans. They also played an important role as moneychangers, converting rice into money, and even lending money to the *daimyo* against delivery of rice crops. A result of all this trade was that the merchants became very powerful economically.

MONEY was hardly ever used by the majority of people. Instead, people relied on trade. They would trade goods for rice, or sometimes swapped valuable objects, such as musical instruments or clothes, for the things, or services they needed.

Using money was complicated, as gold, silver, copper and iron were all used for making coins in different parts of the country. For example, gold was used in the city of Edo, but in Osaka and Kyoto silver coins were more common. For everyday purchases in shops most people used small copper coins which they kept tucked into the folds of their kimono.

flag at the stern bearing the name of the ship

rudder

hold for storing cargo of soya beans or sake

◁ *One of the main shipping lines was the Higaki, or 'diamond line', so called because of the diamond shape pattern on the ship. The pattern was made by bamboo poles which were crossed over the cargo, to stop it from falling overboard.*

A rich, cultural life

In early Japanese history, music and dance were often associated with religious ceremonies. Gradually, music and dance became accepted forms of entertainment. In the Heian period, music from Korea, China and India was also popular in court.

IN THE HEIAN COURT, music and dance were very important to the nobles. They were an essential part of court rituals and everyday life. An educated person was expected to know how to dance, or play a musical instrument. It was also believed that if a person danced, played or sang well, they would reveal their true character.

MAKE A DECORATIVE SHAMISEN

You will need: string, brown paint, masking tape, cream paper, white card, pencil, scissors, glue

1 For the body, cut two x 20 cm rounded card squares. Cut four card rectangles 20 cm x 6 cm. Tape three to one square, making an open box.

2 For the neck, cut two lengths of card: one 72 cm long x 4 cm at one end and 8 cm at the other; the other 60 cm long x 8 cm at one end and 16 cm at the other. Draw five lines along the short length. Score with scissors and bend to shape. Tape neck pieces together and fix to body as shown above.

3 Add last rectangle and square to close up the body. For the peg head, cut two shapes from card as above. Make three slits in each. For the tuning pegs, cut three strips of card. Pass through the slits and glue in place. For the fret, cut a thick piece of card 4 cm long and glue across top of neck.

MUSIC AND DANCE played an important part in village festivals. A whole village would gather to sing folk songs and dance. Often the songs and dances were special to that region of Japan. Men and women would dance in circles, while other members of the village played flutes and drums, or sometimes the *shamisen*.

FOLK SONGS have a long history in Japanese music. From the Kamakura period, groups of blind minstrels would wander the country singing tales of famous battles. The *'Tales of Heike'* was famous and told the story of two powerful families, the Taira and the Minamoto clans, who fought during the 12th century. Minstrels played on a type of lute called a *biwa* while singing these tales to their audience.

◁ *Drums of all sizes are used to accompany traditional music at festivals throughout Japan.*

THE SHAMISEN came to Japan from Okinawa in the late 1500s. At first the *shamisen* was played by blind lute players, but it quickly became a favourite instrument in the entertainment districts of cities. It was widely used in **Kabuki** theatre and by female entertainers called *geisha*, and was also popular with ordinary townspeople.

GEISHA were women trained from an early age to entertain by singing, dancing, playing the *shamisen* and even talking in a witty and elegant manner. Famous *geisha* were like film stars and their skills at music and dance were greatly appreciated. They often had several maids who might also be training to become *geisha*.

4 Slide the peg head over the end of the neck and glue in position.

5 For a bridge, cut an arched rectangle of card 8 cm x 4 cm, as above. Make three holes in the top of the arch. Now glue to end of the body. Paint the *shamisen* brown.

6 Cut a large square of cream paper and glue over the body.

7 Tie three strings to the tuning pegs. Pass the strings over the fret and tie to the bridge at the end of the *shamisen* body.

8 To make the plectrum, cut shapes out of the white card as shown above. Tape the pieces together and paint yellow.

— tuning pegs

— fret

— peg head

— neck

body

plectrum

bridge

◁ *The shamisen has three strings which are strummed. It is used to accompany chanters in a type of theatre known as* **Bunraku**.

⊖ **NOH THEATRE** has its origins in rituals that were connected with the rice harvest, and with entertainment in Buddhist temples.

In a performance, the actor moves in a slow, elegant fashion across an almost bare stage. Four musicians sit at the back of the stage and accompany a group of people who chant a story in a solemn way. This chant tells a story as the performance unfolds. The main character in the story often wears a mask which represents a certain type of person, perhaps a young man, or maybe a ghost. The expression on the mask tells the audience if the character is sad, jealous, or angry.

Originally, Noh theatre was not intended for ordinary people, but was only for the nobles and samurai. It became so popular among some high-ranking lords that they would invite Noh actors to their homes to perform, and would even take part in the performance themselves.

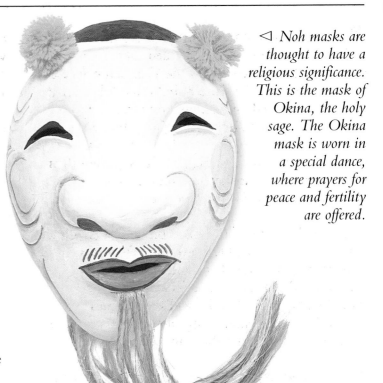

◁ *Noh masks are thought to have a religious significance. This is the mask of Okina, the holy sage. The Okina mask is worn in a special dance, where prayers for peace and fertility are offered.*

⊖ MAKE A NOH MASK

You will need: paint, paintbrush, sandpaper, strips of newspaper, wallpaper paste, string, wool, masking tape, balloon

1 Blow up the balloon. Cover one half with several layers of newspaper strips soaked in the paste. Use the paper and paste to form a nose.

2 When the mask is dry, pop the balloon and smooth any rough edges with sandpaper. Cut out two holes for the eyes, half-way up the mask.

🐸 **BUNRAKU** was a form of theatre, popular during the Edo period. The stars of Bunraku were not actors, but half life-sized puppets. While the puppets provided all the movements on stage, someone off-stage sang in a chant-like way, telling the story and providing the voices of the puppets.

TWO OR THREE PUPPET MASTERS, dressed in black, controlled the movements of the puppets on stage. The puppets made all kinds of happy and sad expressions, as even their eyeballs and eyebrows could be moved. A musician would play the *shamisen* to accompany the voices of the chanters.

ACCORDING TO LEGEND, Kabuki theatre began in 1586 when an entertainer called Okuni danced in a dry river bed in Kyoto. By the 17th century, it had become very popular. The Kabuki that Okuni had created was played by women, and often their dancing was so shocking that fighting broke out among the audience. As a result, the authorities banned women from taking part. Young men then took their place, but the same problems with the audience occured. So, they too were banned.

Finally, Kabuki was allowed to continue with adult male actors. They had to shave their forelocks to show they had come of age and convince the authorities that they were serious artists. The actors took on all the female roles and soon became so skilled that their beautiful appearance and costumes often set the style for fashion in the cities.

▷ *Kabuki actors start their training at a very early age. They have to learn all the roles and every aspect of Kabuki movement, make-up and costume.*

THE ENTRANCES AND EXITS of a Kabuki actor were very exciting. The actors were famous for striking dramatic poses; flinging their heads and arms around and stamping their feet. Some costumes were designed to look over-sized and colourful, to give the actor a larger-than-life presence on stage.

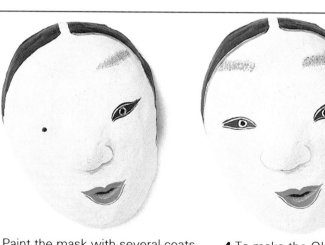

3 Paint the mask with several coats of white paint. When the paint has dried, draw the outline of the eyes and nose in black, and the lips in red.

4 To make the Okina mask opposite, add tufts of wool for eyebrows, and bits of string to make a beard.

KABUKI PERFORMANCES were very lively and colourful, recounting tales from Japanese history, adventures of superhuman heroes, as well as love stories and tales of ordinary life in the town. During the play, members of the audience would shout out words of praise, or even rude comments, to the actors on stage.

THE NOBLES had a great deal of free time during the Heian period. Games and sports were an important way for them to amuse themselves, although some games and sports were more than just entertainment. **Sumo** wrestling contained important rituals which were part of Shinto belief; the referee even wore the costume of a Shinto priest. Other sports were practised for very practical reasons. **Martial arts**, such as **karate**, **kendo** and **judo**, were developed to help a warrior improve the skills he needed in battle. As well as developing physical fitness, all of the martial arts required strong concentration and mental discipline.

KENDO, which means 'the way of the sword', was developed so that the samurai could keep up with sword-practice. By the 14th century there were several schools teaching kendo. The spontaneous moves and rituals of kendo went hand-in-hand with the Zen Buddhist idea of *mushin*, or 'no mind'. Rivals moved so quickly that they did not have time to think, but had to rely on their reflexes.

⚔ MAKE A KENDO MASK

You will need: card, glue, black felt, paint (black, gold, red), needle and thread, scissors

1 Cut two or three long strips of card, 3 cm wide and glue them together.

2 Curve the strip into an oval that is large enough to fit over your face.

3 Cut a strip that is longer than the oval and 3 cm wide. Glue it along the oval, so that it curves out, as above.

4 Glue short strips across the oval, curving them outwards, as above.

5 Paint the oval shape red and the other strips black. When dry, paint a gold line on top of each black strip.

SUMO WRESTLING is the most ancient sport in Japan. Originally, wrestlers fought in a small ring in Shinto shrines during festivals. The object was to make the opponent touch the ground with a part of his body, other than his feet, or fall out of the ring. From about 1780, meetings were held over 10 days, and wrestlers were ranked according to their ability. Eventually, sumo stadiums were built, and popular wrestlers became as famous as some Kabuki actors.

◁ *Shinto rituals play an important part in sumo: a wrestler must wear his hair and belt in a precise way.*

△ *Opponents sit in this crouching position before and after combat.*

◁ *This position is good for both attack and defence.*

IN KENDO TODAY, instead of using a sword, a long bamboo pole called a *shinai* is used. Those who practise kendo are known as *kendo-ka*. Action is so swift, that it is impossible to prepare moves in advance.

◁ *The 'cut' is a position of attack.*

6 For the hood, place two pieces of black felt together. Cut out the shape as shown above. Place the mask on the felt and cut around it to make the correct size hole for your face.

7 Sew both pieces of felt together along the back of the hood.

8 Turn the hood inside out. Glue the mask to the inside edge of the hood, or sew for extra strength.

△ *It is important to hold the shinai with a firm grip.*

🐸 **JUDO**, 'the way of gentleness', comes from a martial art called *ju-jitsu* which involves opponents trying to wrestle each other to the ground. It started as a form of unarmed self-defence and was popular in the late Edo period. By 1911 it was widely taught in schools all over Japan.

KARATE did not actually reach mainland Japan until the 1920s. Originating in China, the word *karate* means 'empty hand'. The fists and feet are used for fighting, instead of weapons.

◁ ▷ *While sparring, opponents keep their eyes constantly trained on one another.*

A living language

Nobody is very sure where the Japanese language comes from. One theory is that it is related to Korean; another is that it originates from a group of languages that come from central Asia. The way Japanese was spoken varied from region to region. In northern Japan, the Ainu people spoke a language that was totally different from Japanese.

 UNTIL THE SEVENTH CENTURY, the Japanese had no way of writing their own language. During the Heian period, they looked to China in order to develop a writing system. With Chinese characters, the Japanese were able to enrich their own language and record their ideas.

HANKO are special stamps which were originally made from jade or ivory. Characters representing a person's name are carved into one end. The hanko is dipped in ink and used to sign important documents.

MAKE A HANKO

You will need: orange paint, paper, felt-tip pen, sharp knife, potato

1 Ask an adult to cut the potato in half. Draw one of the characters on the right on the potato.

2 Ask an adult to help you cut around the character. Remove the unmarked bits of potato, so that the character stands out.

3 Paint the character and press it firmly on to a piece of ordinary paper, or special Japanese paper, to make a print.

▷ *These two characters read 'Yamada', a fairly common name in Japan. Today, words of Chinese origin still make up more than half of all Japanese words.*

 CALLIGRAPHY, the art of handwriting, has been popular in Japan since the Heian period. At first, calligraphy was used to record Buddhist prayers and famous Chinese sayings and poems. The style and techniques used to produce beautiful texts were greatly appreciated, in the same way that a painting might be admired. Special brushes were dipped in black ink and a poem, or another piece of writing, was copied on to delicately coloured sheets of paper. The way the words looked on the paper was just as important as what they said.

◁ *This girl is using calligraphy brushes to write a letter.*

FOR MANY CENTURIES, scholars and officials used the Chinese language for writing. However, the Japanese language, when spoken, sounded very different from Chinese, and Chinese characters were complicated and took a long time to write. A new system of writing was needed to record Japanese sounds, and to simplify Chinese characters. A set of syllables called *kana*, which were originally based on Chinese, gradually evolved. Each *kana* syllable could be used to represent a Japanese sound. Over time, two sets of *kana* came into being, one called *hiragana*, and the other called *katakana* and so, along with Chinese characters, there were three ways of writing. Sometimes, all three can be found within one sentence.

△ *Prayers written on strips of paper are often hung around Shinto shrines for good luck.*

yama

da

JAPANESE LITERATURE began to appear shortly after the writing system was introduced. The earliest known piece of writing is 'The Kojiki', or 'record of ancient matters'. It describes the birth of Emperor Jimmu and the creation of the Japanese islands.

THE FIRST POEMS date from the end of the eighth century. The '*Man'yoshu*' is a collection of about 4,500 poems divided into 20 books. One of the themes of the poems is a warning that life is very short and soon over.

BY THE END OF THE 17TH CENTURY, many people were able to enjoy reading plays, stories and poetry. This was due to more advanced methods of printing and people being able to borrow books from libraries.

木 = *tree*

山 = *mountain*

川 = *river*

田 = *rice field*

人 = *person*

口 = *mouth*

△ *Chinese characters developed from simple drawings. Gradually the drawings developed and became the characters that are used today.*

Arts and crafts

Although China was a major influence on arts and crafts in Japan, the Japanese created their own sense of style. They made many beautiful paintings and **ceramics** which reflected Japanese history and culture. It was also important that even simple, everyday objects were made with great care.

 THE ART OF PAPER-MAKING arrived in Japan from Korea in the seventh century. The Japanese soon found many ways to put paper to good use. Not only was it used as a writing material, but its lightness and strength made it a practical and often beautiful building material. It was also used for religious purposes, for writing prayers and marking sacred places with prayers written on strips.

PAPER MAKING

You will need: wood, muslin, staple gun, staples, hacksaw, baking tray, food liquidizer, strips of white paper, flower petals, grass, hammer, nails

1 Ask an adult to cut eight lengths of wood, four x 18 cm and four x 22 cm.

2 Ask an adult to help you make two rectangular frames by nailing the lengths of wood together.

3 Stretch the muslin over one frame and fix it with the staple gun. You now have a screen and a deckle (lid).

4 To make the pulp, tear the paper into small squares and soak in water overnight. Mash or liquidize the paper until it looks like porridge.

5 For colour, add some shredded flower petals and grass to the pulp.

△ *This 17th-century, hand-painted screen is made of paper.*

DURING THE EDO PERIOD, the wives of fishermen and farmers made work clothes out of paper. They used a special type of paper, called *shifu*, which was made from twisted paper woven into strips. A finer version of *shifu* was also used to make tablecloths, handkerchiefs and even mosquito netting.

PAPER PRODUCTION became a big industry during this time. Different regions specialized in producing paper for specific purposes. Paper was needed for writing letters, printing books and making woodblock prints. It was also used for everyday things: sliding screens inside houses were made of paper, as were windows, lanterns and fans. Some clothes were made of paper, such as the *kamiko* worn by Buddhist monks. Parasols were made of oiled paper that was waterproof. Before the Heian period, parasols were carried by warriors, monks and nobles for protection against the sun and rain.

THE TEXTURE, COLOUR AND DESIGN of paper were all very important points to consider when writing a letter, or creating a piece of calligraphy. During this period, paper designs became very intricate. Paper was dyed with blue, white, violet, indigo and brown inks that were blended to form interesting shapes. Gold or silver patterns were sometimes printed on it, and even fine metal flakes were mixed into the paper.

THE PERSONALITY OF A WRITER was judged not only by the content of the letter, but also by the kind of paper he or she used. Therefore, anyone sending a letter would spend a long time carefully choosing the type and colour of the paper, and practising their calligraphy. Whoever received the letter could tell whether the writer had good taste or not.

6 Add more water and stir. Place the deckle on top of the screen and scoop some pulp into it.

7 Hold both the screen and deckle. Lift them both out of the pulp without tilting them. Gently shake from side to side so that the pulp spreads evenly.

8 To dry the paper, remove the deckle as shown left. Lie the muslin screen with the layer of pulp on it face down on a damp cloth. Use another cloth to mop up excess water on the muslin. The pulp should stick to the damp cloth; then you can gently peel the pulp and cloth away from the muslin screen.

9 Pin the cloth and layer of pulp up to dry, or leave it in an airing cupboard. When dry, lie the cloth face down and peel it away from the sheet of paper.

◁ *To make coloured or patterned paper, add blades of grass, flower petals, or torn pieces of coloured paper.*

THE ART OF WRAPPING PRESENTS has always been very important in Japan. Before paper was commonly used, gifts were wrapped in fine cloth. There are still many special rules about how gifts should be wrapped; it is considered very poor taste not to wrap a present correctly.

LACQUER is a type of resin which comes from the lacquer tree, found in the northern parts of Japan. It was used on all kinds of objects, from tables to writing boxes, and vases to hair ornaments, to give them a hard, glossy appearance. Gold lacquerware was also used at banquets.

TO LACQUER AN OBJECT, it was first coated with lac, the sap collected from the lacquer tree. A piece of linen was placed on top of the layer of lac, and several more coats were brushed on. When the layers were dry, the surface was polished many times to give a shiny, black appearance.

MAKE A LACQUERED BENTO BOX

You will need: scissors, thick card, masking tape, glue, paints (red, black, gold), varnish

1 Cut three squares from the card: base: 17 cm, lid: 18 cm, inside lid: 16.5 cm. For the side panels, cut eight rectangles: four measuring 17 x 6.5 cm and four 16.5 x 6.5 cm.

2 Glue matching side panels together for extra strength.

3 Tape all the pieces together, as shown above, to make a box. For the lid, glue the smaller square to the underside of the larger one.

4 Paint the outside of both the lid and the box black. Leave to dry.

5 Now paint the inside of the box and lid red, then leave to dry.

WOODBLOCKS were used for printing in Japan as long ago as the eighth century. The use of woodblock printing probably came from China and was first introduced by Buddhists, who used the blocks to print prayers and charms.

WOODBLOCK PRINTS in the 17th century showed the glamorous lives of *geisha*, actors and sumo wrestlers. The world in which these famous people lived was so different from everyday life, that it was called *ukiyo*, or 'floating world'.

MAKE A WOODBLOCK PRINT

You will need: craft knife, pencil, 4 polystyrene tiles, tracing paper, felt-tip pen, paint, paper, strong glue

1 Glue all four tiles together.

2 Draw the frog on the tracing paper. Place the trace on the tiles. Go over the trace with a pencil to leave an impression on the tiles. Go over the impression with a felt-tip.

3 Ask an adult to help you cut out the frog using a craft knife. Cut through the top two layers of the tiles so that your design stands out in relief.

AT THE END OF THE HEIAN PERIOD, new techniques in lacquerware were created. In one particular technique, tiny pieces of real gold and silver were sprinkled on to the lacquer while it was still wet.

6 Use gold paint to decorate the box. When the paint is dry, varnish the box to give it a laquered look.

AN ARTIST, ENGRAVER AND PRINTER were needed to make woodblock prints. The artist made the original drawing; an engraver carved the drawing into the wood and the printer applied the inks to the blocks and printed the image on paper.

4 Paint the raised surfaces with different coloured paints. While the paint is still wet, turn the tile over and press it on to the paper to make a print.

DURING THE 17TH CENTURY, trade in porcelain and lacquerware became very important between Japan and Europe. Thousands of bowls, chests and objects of art coated in lacquer, or decorated with mother-of-pearl or ivory, were shipped to Europe.

LACQUERED WRITING BOXES, decorated with mother-of-pearl, or gold, were highly prized possessions for the Heian nobility. But, by the Edo period, these objects of art did not only belong to the privileged nobles and samurai. Ordinary people, who had perhaps become wealthy through trade, also wanted to buy beautiful objects to keep in their homes. Many people started to buy woodblock prints and, because they were almost as cheap as a bowl of noodles, it meant that most people could afford to buy a piece of art.

▽ *This woodblock print is copied from an 18th-century design called 'Frog', by Matsumoto Hoji. You could use your hanko to sign your print.*

△ *An origami crane.*

ORIGAMI, or paper folding, originated with the Shinto religion at the end of the Heian period. Figures of Shinto gods were made from paper and hung around shrines. It is thought that the first piece of origami was made by Fujiwara no Kiyosuke, a man who folded paper into the shape of a frog.

IN THE KAMAKURA PERIOD, nobles would attach a piece of origami to their swords to bring them luck in battle. Later, in the Muromachi period, special schools were opened to teach people the art of origami. As paper became more readily available, the art of paper-folding became a popular pastime for many ordinary people.

MAKE AN ORIGAMI FLAPPING BIRD

| *a* | *b* | *c* | *d* | *e* | *f* |

You will need: square piece of paper

1 Fold the paper in half along the two diagonals. Unfold, turn the paper over and fold in half horizontally, then vertically. Make the creases very sharp. Unfold the paper as in *a.*

2 Fold the paper in half horizontally.

3 Hold both sets of corners and push all four corners inwards as in *b,* to make a star shape.

4 Lie flat in a square shape, *c,* with the opening at the bottom.

5 Fold the edges of the top layer in towards the centre crease, *d.*

6 Fold the top triangle down over the two triangles at the front, *e.*

7 Pull out the two folded triangles again, as in *f.*

8 Now, take hold of the bottom point and lift up the top layer of paper. Pull it up and back as in *g.*

△ *This porcelain dish was made in the town of Arita where the first Japanese porcelain was made.*

POTTERY was used in Japan as early as 800–300 BC. Early pottery was made of clay that was kneaded into basic pots for storing food. In the 16th century, Korean potters who came to Japan changed the style of Japanese ceramics. They set up kilns on the island of Kyushu and helped to create styles which later influenced the production of porcelain in Arita.

FROM THE 16TH CENTURY, tea bowls that were designed for use in the tea ceremony were considered valuable possessions. Some bowls were made to look old. A famous teacher of the tea ceremony, Sen no Rikyu, asked a tile maker to design a simple tea bowl. He made a plain bowl, such as a peasant might use. This simple style of pottery became known as *raku.*

IKEBANA, or flower arranging, has its roots in both the Shinto and Buddhist religions, where flowers were presented as offerings to gods. In the 15th century, a style of *ikebana* called *rikka* was introduced. Trees, shrubs and flowers were arranged in a way that reflected a scene from the natural landscape. In the home, people used more simple arrangements with only one type of plant or flower. The longest flower represented heaven and the future, the second represented man and the present, while the third represented the earth and the past.

▷ *Some ikebana arrangements have special meanings: both bamboo and pine are symbols of good luck.*

| *g* | *h* | *i* | *j* | *k* | *l* | *m* |

9 Pull the corner right up and flatten out the diamond shape as in *h*.

10 Turn the whole shape over, *i*.

11 Repeat steps five to nine on this side. This will give you a long thin diamond shape with a smaller triangle hidden in the middle, *j*.

11 Fold the bottom triangles up and outwards, below the centre crease, *k*.

12 Fold the triangles back down. Open the diamond at the sides and tuck the triangles up inbetween the folds, *l*.

13 For the head, turn the tip of one of the triangles over as in *m*.

14 Pull the upper parts of the triangle apart and fold downwards to form the wings.

15 Hold the flaps underneath your bird and pull them gently backwards and forwards.

MANY DIFFERENT SHAPES AND STYLES can be made in origami, from simple cubes to animals such as monkeys or rabbits. A very popular shape to make is the crane, which is the symbol of long life and good fortune. When people wish for something special, they sometimes fold hundreds, or even thousands of cranes and thread them on to long lengths of string. Then they hang the cranes outside Shinto shrines as offerings to the spirits.

▷ *The most important aspect of origami is that the paper is always folded – it is never glued or cut. Some of the best designs are also the most simple, while others are very complicated.*

Nature's laws

Throughout history, different religious beliefs have existed side-by-side in Japan. Families were happy to combine them in their daily lives, depending on their needs. The Shinto religion was used for births and marriages. But for matters concerning death, for example when remembering, or praying for dead members of the family, people followed Buddhist teachings. Confucianism, which originally came from China, provided strict guidelines for behaviour within society. It stressed the importance of treating elders with respect, and loyalty to one's rulers.

△ *The entrances to sacred Shinto shrines were marked by tall, wooden gates called torii, which were sometimes painted red.*

SHINTO means 'the way of the gods' and is the oldest form of religion in Japan. Shinto followers believe in the worship of spirits called **kami**. These spirits are thought to live in the sky, islands, waterfalls, mountains and tall trees. Mount Fuji, the highest mountain in Japan, is believed to be sacred. Some animals are sacred because they are thought to be the messengers of the *kami*.

THE SHINTO RELIGION has no sacred scriptures or set of rules. It developed from a mixture of folk tales and legends from the earliest days of Japanese history. A respect for nature has always been very important in Shinto. People tried to keep the local *kami* happy with offerings of food and drink, so as to ensure a successful harvest and to protect themselves from bad luck.

MAKE A SHINTO SHRINE

You will need: two cardboard boxes, thin wooden dowel, four wooden lollipop sticks, brown paint, masking tape, PVA glue, craft knife

1 Turn one box over to form a base. Ask an adult to help you cut a house shape from the second box. Glue in position as above. Cut 20 lengths of dowel and glue around base of shrine, leaving a space for the stairs.

2 For the rail, cut five varying lengths of dowel to rest on top of the upright dowels (leaving a gap for the stairs). Glue in place.

3 For the roof, cut two large sections of cardboard and glue them in place.

4 Cut a length of dowel the same length as the roof and glue along the ridge of the roof.

5 For the stairs, cut a long strip of cardboard. Double back part of the strip for a ridged effect, as shown right. Glue the stairs at an angle to the first floor as above.

6 Glue two lengths of dowel to the base of the stairs. Cut two pieces of card for the porch roof and glue to the shrine wall and posts. Stick a length of dowel along the ridge of the porch.

THROUGHOUT MOST OF THE HEIAN PERIOD, Shinto was the main religion practised, particularly in the countryside and at the Heian court. People were very superstitious; anything to do with death, illness, or blood was to be avoided at all costs. If someone fell ill or died, bits of willow-wood were hung from houses as a warning to keep away.

THE SHINTO SHRINES AT ISE are the most sacred shrines in Japan and date back to the fourth or fifth century. Until the 15th century they were visited only by members of the imperial family, but later they became a popular place of pilgrimage for many Japanese. One of the shrines is dedicated to the sun goddess Amaterasu. According to Shinto belief, the rulers of Japan are supposed to be descended from this goddess.

DURING THE EDO PERIOD, pilgrimages to famous shrines and temples became very popular. Some people saw them as a good excuse to travel with friends. Others went on pilgrimages to ask for special favours, or to thank the *kami* if their family had received good fortune.

△ *Daikoku, on the left, is a Shinto god of luck. He carries a mallet for grinding rice and is associated with the rice harvest. Inari (the fox) on the right, is one of the most popular kami in Japan today. The red cloth is a sign that the kami is being taken care of. People make offerings of food and drink to the kami to keep them happy.*

7 Make two cross shapes from lollipop sticks. Glue a cross to the front and back of the roof ridge. Then fix three short pieces of dowel across the middle of the ridge as shown above. Paint your shrine brown.

▷ *This shinto shrine is based on the shrines at Ise.*

BUDDHISM is a religion that spread to Japan from China and Korea in the sixth century. It began in India with the teachings of Buddha, a man who lived from 563-483 BC. He achieved **enlightenment**, a perfect mental and physical state, and spent the rest of his life teaching his disciples.

▷ *As Buddhism spread throughout Japan, many new temples were built with a pagoda. Underneath the pagoda, relics of Buddha, such as pieces of clothing that he may have worn, were buried.*

upper stories used to view surrounding area

wooden Japanese pagoda

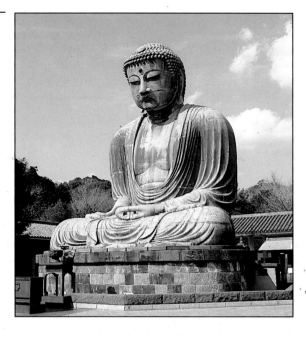

△ *The Great Buddha at Kamakura was built in 1252. The statue is made of bronze and stands 11.5 metres high.*

DURING THE SIXTH CENTURY, Prince Shotoku encouraged the growth of Buddhism in Japan. The rulers of Japan were attracted to Buddhism because they thought that the whole country would be protected from danger if they followed this religion. Many temples were built throughout the country so that monks and nuns could study and teach.

IN THE HEIAN PERIOD, Buddhism became increasingly popular. The nobles at court found the complex beliefs even more challenging than Shinto. By the late 12th century, Buddhism had reached ordinary people. They were comforted by the belief that anyone could reach paradise by calling out to the Buddha to save them.

ZEN BUDDHISM was introduced to Japan in the late 12th and 13th centuries by a monk called Eisai, who had studied in China. Zen had some very strict practices. Monks would **meditate** for many hours, sometimes receiving sharp blows with a stick to help them concentrate more fully. It was also believed that you could meditate while doing everyday tasks such as cleaning, or even eating.

✖ **THE STRICT DISCIPLINE** that was needed to follow Zen Buddhism made the religion popular among the samurai. They were attracted by the calmness of the religion, the strict meditation routines and the possibility of enlightenment. The samurai used many of these ideas to help them become fearless fighters, unafraid of death.

Zen ideas also had a strong influence on art and culture. In times of unrest, artists and scholars took refuge in temples and monasteries. As a result, Zen arts, such as gardening, calligraphy, ink painting and the tea ceremony, flourished in these centres.

✖ ⌣ **THE TEA CEREMONY** was practised by Zen monks. Originally, they drank tea to help them stay alert when they meditated. Gradually, making tea became an art form. The monks would pay attention to every detail of the tea-making, from boiling the water, to the way the tea master whisked the tea in the tea bowls. Later on, ordinary people practised the ceremony: they relaxed and meditated in the quiet atmosphere and forgot their normal lives. Similar ideas lay behind the design of Zen gardens.

△ *Water is incorporated into many Zen gardens to suggest a waterfall, ocean, or a fast-flowing river. Or else it may simply provide a soothing sound as it drips into a stone basin.*

✖ **ZEN GARDENS** were designed with Zen beliefs in mind. Sometimes water or flowers were used, or dry landscapes were created using moss, stones, gravel and sand. Often the gravel was carefully raked into swirling patterns. An onlooker was supposed to imagine what all the different shapes in the garden might be. For example, rocks might represent mountains, or raked gravel could be a whirlpool, or waves on the sea or a river.

✖ **MAKE A ZEN GARDEN**

4 Add the stones and moss to complete your miniature Zen garden.

You will need: cardboard box, thin dowelling, plastic comb, small rocks, moss (from a florist's shop), sand, craft knife, glue

1 Cut down the sides of the cardboard box to make a shallow tray, as above.

2 Ask an adult to cut a section of comb. Glue the comb to one end of the dowel. Pour a layer of sand in the tray and shake gently until smooth.

3 Rake curved patterns in the sand, as above.

△ *You could add a small water feature to your garden.*

Japan in the modern age

Japan is now home to over 123 million people, which is the seventh largest population in the world. Much of the country is mountainous, so flatter areas are very densely populated. Most people live in very modern cities with skyscrapers and well-organized public transport. As one of the most technologically advanced countries in the world, Japan has an enormous influence on global economy. However, tradition still plays an important role in society.

FESTIVALS are an important part of the Japanese year. People still gather to see the cherry blossoms and have picnics under the trees, just as the Heian nobles did. Carp streamers and dolls are put on display for Children's Day in May and for the Doll's festival in March.

▽ *The tea ceremony is still an important ritual in Japan today.*

△ *This park in Tokyo is crowded with people enjoying the cherry blossom.*

TRADITIONAL JAPANESE ARTS are studied at special schools. Many women, at some time or other, study an ancient art, such as *ikebana* or the tea ceremony. Although most Japanese wear 'western-style' clothes, at weddings and other formal occasions, they often swap their suits, or jeans and T-shirts, for kimono.

OLD SKILLS often go hand-in-hand with new ones. At school, children learn subjects, such as science and foreign languages, which will serve them in the modern age. But the ancient skill of calligraphy is still vital, as pupils have to learn to write up to 2,000 characters before they leave school.

△ *Traditional style interiors are much admired in Japan.*

AS BUILDING LAND IS SCARCE, houses are often expensive and fairly small, especially in the cities. Some aspects of Japanese architecture have not changed since early times: a modern flat may have one traditional Japanese room, with a *tokonoma*, *tatami* and sliding paper doors. But the other rooms are more likely to be furnished in the Western style.

△ *The Shinkansen, or bullet train, links Tokyo with Kyoto and Osaka, passing Mount Fuji on the way.*

JAPAN IS A LEADER in the manufacture of cars, railway technology and in the electronics industry. Some Japanese companies are among the largest in the world, and many more are well-known outside Japan. For over a century, Japan has been trading openly with other countries – mainly with its Asian neighbours, the USA and Europe.

THE SAMURAI warrior has faded into history, but his legend lives on through comics, film and television. Although the samurai and shoguns no longer exist, Japan still has an emperor who lives in Tokyo, former city of Edo. He symbolizes the state and the unity of the people, although he has no real political power.

OVER THE PAST CENTURY, Japan has changed in many ways. It was once a country whose rulers tried to avoid contact with the outside world. Now it plays a major part in world affairs and its citizens are keen travellers. Japan has also taken on many Western influences – from hamburgers to pop music – yet it has kept a cultural identity that is firmly rooted in its fascinating past.

▽ *Although many Japanese now play baseball and basketball, martial arts have gained in popularity – not only within Japan, but throughout the world.*

Glossary

Ainu A group of people who once lived in northern Honshu and who now live in Hokkaido. They have a different appearance and culture from other Japanese people.

anthropology The study of the culture, language, origins and behaviour of people.

archaeology The study of the remains of buildings and artefacts left behind by people who lived in the past.

Buddhism A religion based on the teachings of Buddha (Gautama Siddhartha) in India in the sixth century BC. Buddhists believe that they can reach a perfect state called enlightenment through meditation.

Bakufu The government set up by the samurai during the times when they held political power.

Bunraku A form of Japanese theatre using puppets that are about half the size of a person.

calligraphy The art of fine handwriting. The characters are written from top to bottom, and right to left across special Japanese paper. Sometimes the paper may be hand-made.

ceramics Objects made from pottery or porcelain. Japan is famous for its ceramic ware, such as *raku*, and some pieces are very valuable.

clan A large family group. For hundreds of years, Japan suffered from a series of clan wars, until single rule was imposed in 1603.

class structure The way in which people in some societies are ranked according to certain attributes, such as wealth or ability.

Confucianism A system of belief founded by Confucius (K'ung-fu-tzu) in China in the fifth century BC. Confucianism sets out a range of rules regarding how a person should behave. These include being loyal to one's country and lord above one's family, and obeying authority without question.

daimyo A powerful Japanese landowner who was also sometimes a military leader.

Edo period The period of Japanese history from 1600 to 1868, named after the city of Edo (Tokyo). It is also called the Tokugawa period.

enlightenment A perfect mental and physical state which Buddhists try to reach by meditating.

geisha A woman trained to entertain through music, dance and witty conversation.

general election An occasion when the people of a country can vote to be represented in the government. They can choose from a selection of candidates of different political parties.

Go A game involving a board marked in a grid and two sets of counters. The object is to cover more space on the board with your counters than your opponent does.

hanko A cylindrical seal with a character carved at one end which is dipped in ink and used to 'sign' documents.

Heian period The period of Japanese history from 790 to 1185, named after the city of Heian, which the Emperor Kammu made his capital.

historian A person who studies and writes about history.

ikebana The art of flower-arranging. It was originally part of Buddhist and Shinto rituals.

judo A martial art in which the contestants try to throw, or wrestle each other to the ground.

Kabuki A form of Japanese theatre in which actors in elaborate costumes and make-up perform using dramatic gestures.

Kamakura period The period of Japanese history from 1185 to 1333. It is named after the place in eastern Japan where the shogun Yoritomo established his military government.

kami Spirits that are worshipped in the Shinto religion. Kami can live in places, objects, animals and people.

karate A martial art that involves fighting with the fists and feet.

ken A measurement used in house-building. One *ken* is the length of a man lying down, that is, about 1.8 metres.

kendo A martial art in which opponents fight using bamboo staffs. Kendo developed from sword fighting and means 'way of the sword'.

kimono A loose-fitting garment tied with a sash which is traditionally worn by Japanese men and women.

lacquer A natural varnish from the lacquer tree used to harden and decorate objects.

martial arts Various kinds of armed and unarmed combat that developed in the East. Japanese forms, such as judo, karate, kendo and sumo, developed from the fighting skills of the samurai warriors.

meditation Spending time thinking deeply and trying not to be influenced by things around you.

Muromachi and Momoyama period
The period of Japanese history from 1392 to 1600. During this time, there were many wars between the different daimyo. Eventually, Japan was brought together under one ruler, Toyotomi Hideyoshi, in 1582.

Noh A form of Japanese theatre which uses dance, mime and masks.

origami The Japanese art of folding paper into interesting or beautiful shapes.

page A boy who becomes a member of a household in order to serve the master and to receive training in return.

political To do with the government of a country and its policy-making.

sake A type of wine made from rice.

samurai A Japanese warrior whose duty was to serve his lord, or daimyo. The samurai were the highest-ranking people in society.

shamisen A lute-like instrument which arrived in Japan in the 16th century. It is used in Bunraku and Kabuki theatre.

Shinto A Japanese religion based on the worship of nature and the spirits of ancestors.

shogun The military rulers of Japan. From the 12th century until 1868, shoguns had more power over the country than emperors.

shogunate The government established by the shogun.

society People living together in an ordered community.

soy sauce A sauce which is made from fermented soya beans and used to season food.

sumo A type of wrestling which originated as a harvest thanksgiving ritual in the Shinto religion. Sumo is the oldest sport in Japan.

sushi A dish made of raw fish, or vegetables, and vinegared rice.

tofu A type of food made from soya milk which sets into a curd.

vinegared rice A sweet, sticky rice used in making sushi. To make it, rice vinegar, sugar and salt are mixed with warm cooked rice.

Zen Buddhism A form of Buddhism involving meditation and self-examination that came to Japan in the Kamakura period. Zen Buddhism is passed directly from teacher to pupil, rather than relying on religious writings.

Index

JAPAN

Andrew Haslam & Clare Doran

Consultant: Heidi Potter, B.A.

TWO-CAN
in association with
WATTS BOOKS

First published in Great Britain in 1995 by
Two-Can Publishing Ltd
346 Old Street
London EC1V 9NQ
in association with
Watts Books
96 Leonard Street
London EC2A 4RH

Series concept and original design: Andrew Haslam
Contributing author: Alexandra Parsons

A catalogue record for this book is available from the British Library.

Hardback ISBN: 1 85434 280 0
Paperback ISBN: 1 85434 281 9
Dewey Decimal Classification 952

Managing Editor: Christine Morley
Editor: Jacqueline McCann
Senior Designer: Helen McDonagh
Art Director: Jill Plank
Deputy Art Director: Carole Orbell
Research: Deborah Kespert
Picture Researcher: Dipika Palmer-Jenkins
Model-makers: Corina Holzherr, Paul Holzherr, Melanie Williams
Additional text: David Eaton

Thanks to Tim at Westpoint Studio and Peter Davies
Models: Robert Blankson, Lester Cotier, Catherine Dawes, Anteneh Elcock, Matthew Guest, Amy Kwan, Ana Ivanovic,
James Moller, Charlotte Walters, Yasmin, Miki Zoric.

Photographic credits: Ancient Art & Architecture Collection: p4 (bl), p41, p54; Chris Uhlenbeck: p9, p17, p33, p34; Helen
McDonagh: map p8; The Hulton-Deutsch Collection: p14; Japan Archive: p57; Japan National Tourist Office: p60; JICC:
p28; Michael Holford: p12, p27; Robert Harding Picture Library: p4 (tr); Tony Stone Worldwide: p46; Victoria & Albert
Museum: covers (edging), p40, p50; Werner Forman Archive: p26; Zefa Photo Library: p20, p24, p34, p38, p42, p58, p61.

All other photographs by Ray Moller
Printed and bound by G. Canale & C. SpA, Turin, Italy

Hardback 2 4 6 8 10 9 7 5 3 1
Paperback 2 4 6 8 10 9 7 5 3 1

To Leonid ~ A B

LITTLE TIGER PRESS LTD,
an imprint of the Little Tiger Group
1 Coda Studios,
189 Munster Road,
London SW6 6AW
www.littletiger.co.uk

First published in Great Britain 2019
This edition published 2019

ISBN 978-1-78881-367-9
LTP/1400/2611/0619
Printed in China
4 6 8 10 9 7 5 3

Aladdin

Anna Bowles

Shahar Kober

LiTTLE TiGER

LONDON

Aladdin was a clever, cheeky boy who lived with
his mother. One day a stranger knocked on their door.
  "I'm your long-lost uncle," he said. "And I'm a magician.
I have a job for you that will make us rich!"

This Little Tiger book
belongs to:

_____

_____

_____

Aladdin's mother didn't remember having a brother. But she was definitely fed up with being poor. So she let Aladdin go.

"We're going to find a precious lamp!" said the magician.

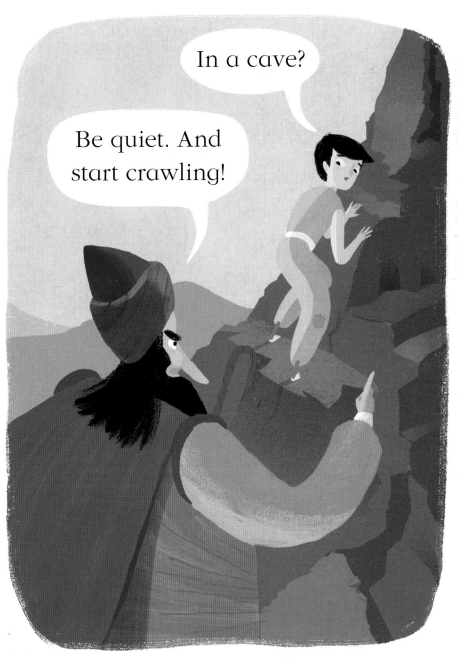

In a cave?

Be quiet. And start crawling!

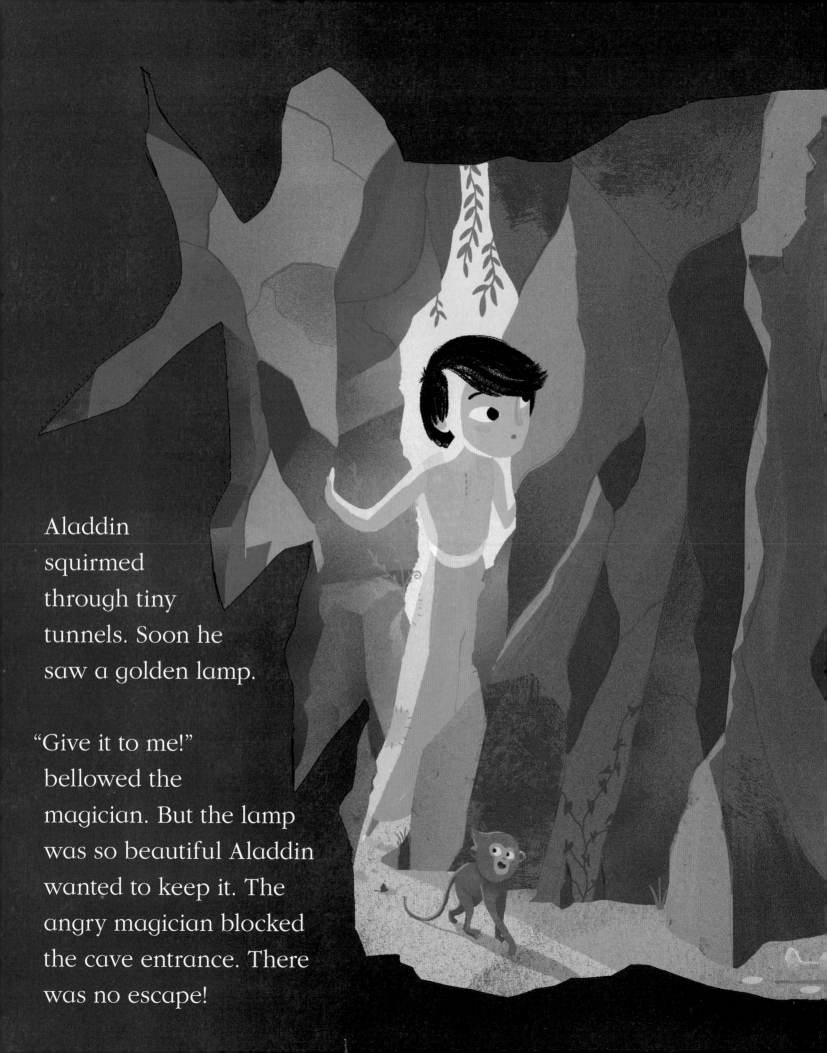

Aladdin squirmed through tiny tunnels. Soon he saw a golden lamp.

"Give it to me!" bellowed the magician. But the lamp was so beautiful Aladdin wanted to keep it. The angry magician blocked the cave entrance. There was no escape!

Aladdin hugged the lamp tight, rubbing it with his hand.

Then something wonderful happened!

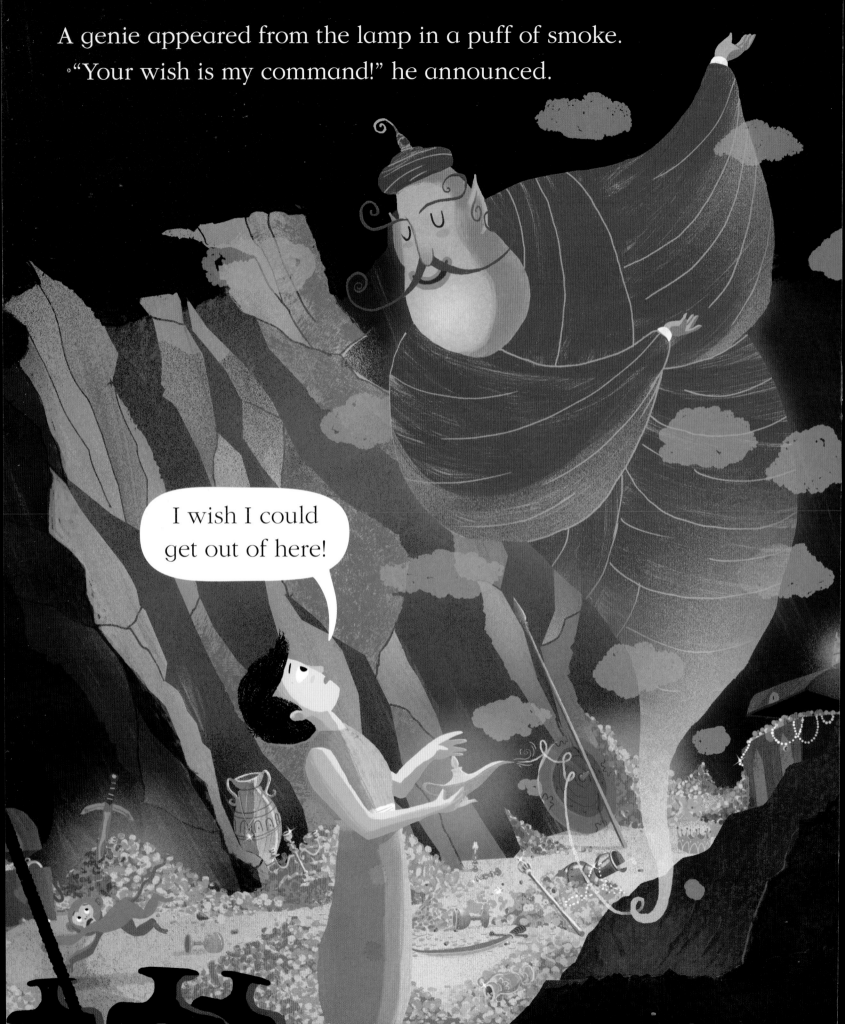

A genie appeared from the lamp in a puff of smoke.
"Your wish is my command!" he announced.

Smoke swirled from the genie's fingers. When it cleared,
Aladdin was standing in a city street.

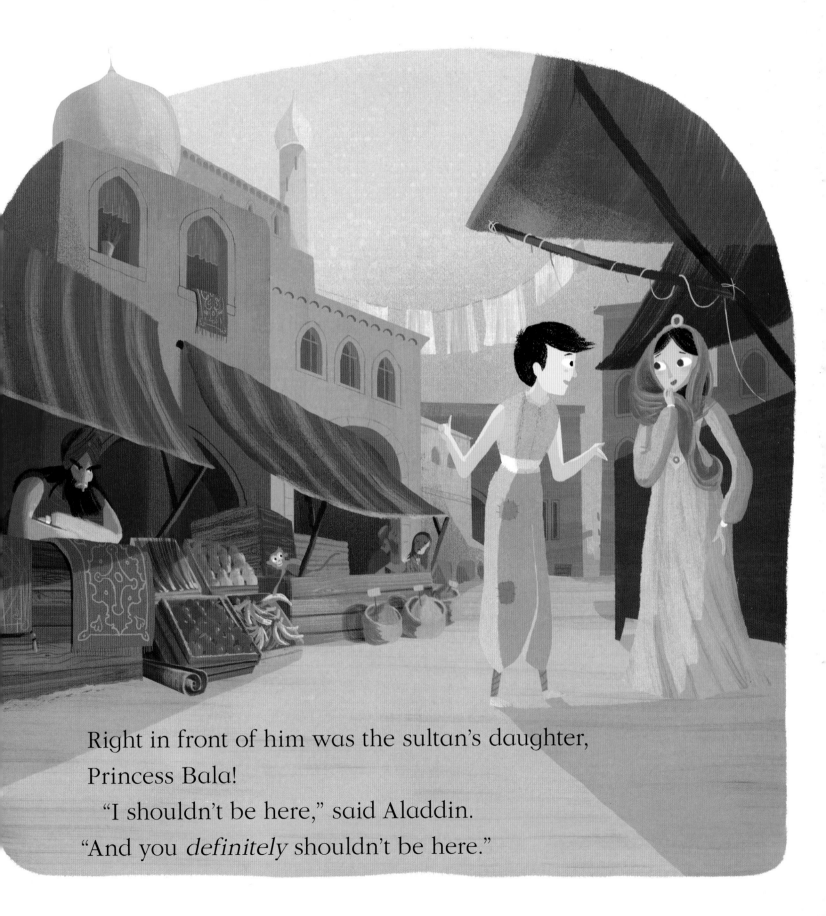

Right in front of him was the sultan's daughter,
Princess Bala!

"I shouldn't be here," said Aladdin.

"And you *definitely* shouldn't be here."

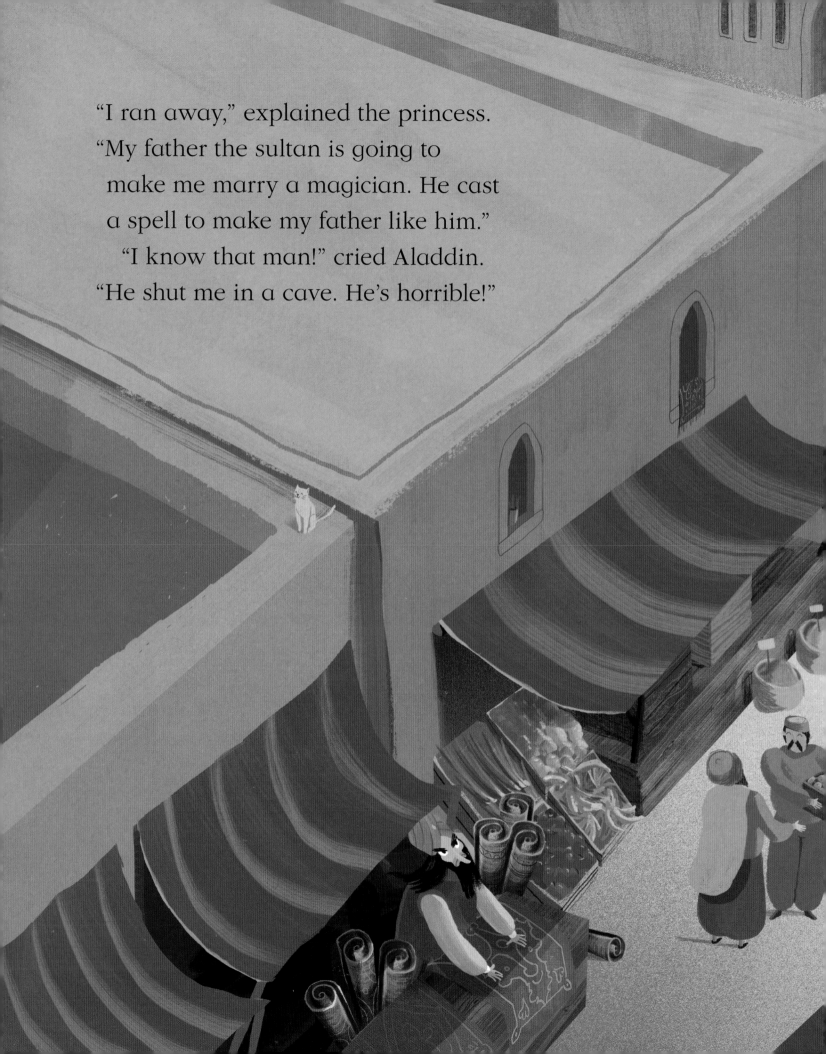

"I ran away," explained the princess.
"My father the sultan is going to
make me marry a magician. He cast
a spell to make my father like him."
"I know that man!" cried Aladdin.
"He shut me in a cave. He's horrible!"

Aladdin and Bala took a magic carpet ride together far above the city and told each other about their troubles. Bala said, "Come to the palace tomorrow. We'll try to reason with my father."

But the next day, as
Aladdin walked to the
palace, the magician
caught him and flung
him into the river.
Aladdin frantically
rubbed the lamp.

"Your wish is my . . ."
began the genie.

Quick! I wish I
was on dry land.

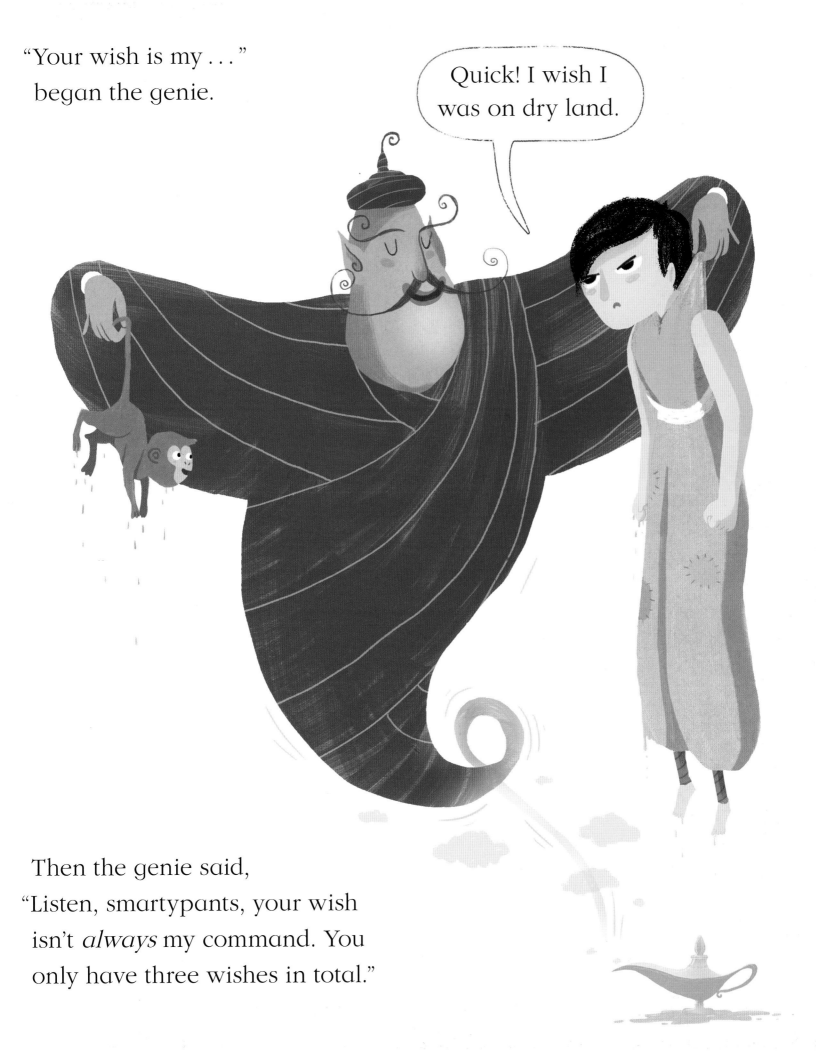

Then the genie said,
"Listen, smartypants, your wish
isn't *always* my command. You
only have three wishes in total."

Meanwhile, inside the palace, the magician was trying everything to make Bala love him.

He gave her flowers.

He wrote her poetry.
(It was awful.)

Finally, he
cast a spell on her.

Aladdin returned and tried to break the spell.
He waved a hand in front of her face. He kissed her cheek.

Then he had an idea. He
caught the magician's stinky
breath in a bottle and made
Bala smell it.

"Urgh!" she cried and went
back to normal.

But while Aladdin was helping
Bala, the magician snatched the
lamp and rubbed it.

"Your wish is . . ." said the genie.

Hang on – you're
not Aladdin. Well, I
suppose you still get
three wishes.

The evil man cried,
"I wish to be the world's
most powerful magician!
I wish I was in charge
instead of the sultan!"

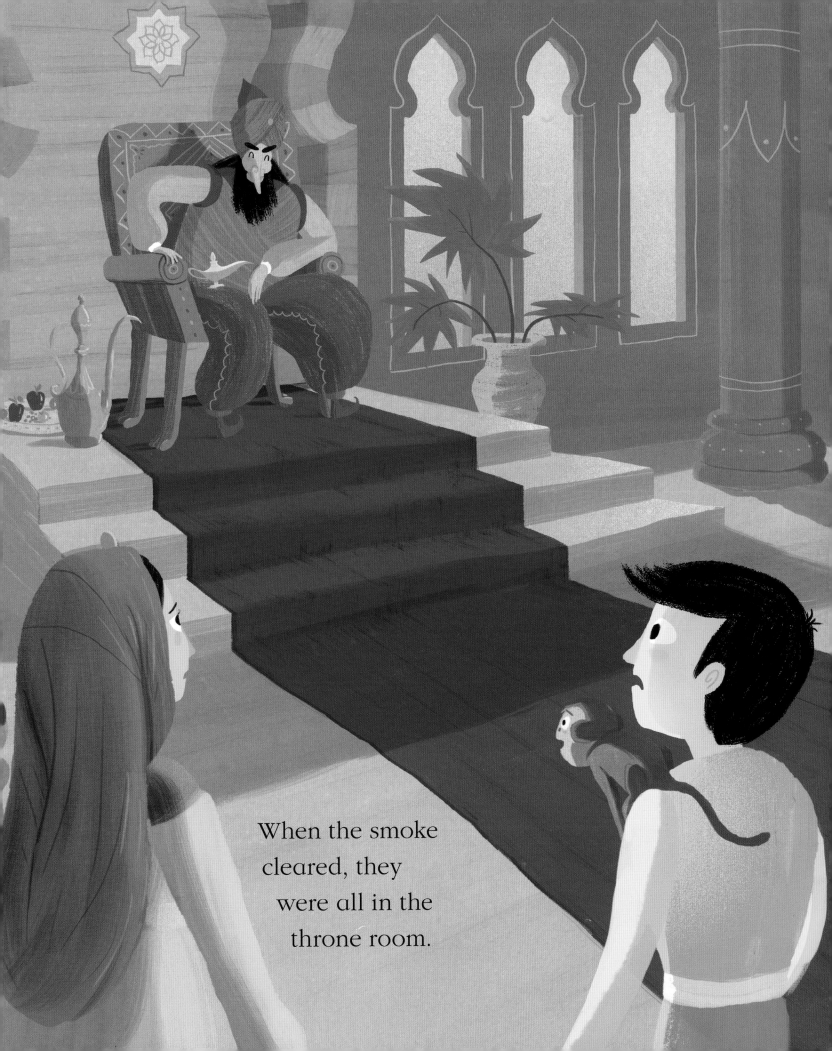

When the smoke cleared, they were all in the throne room.

"My third wish is to make Bala love me," said the magician.

The genie refused!
  "Nuh-uh! I can move stuff around but I can't force people to feel things. Rules are rules."

The magician stamped
and shouted in rage.

Bala crept up behind the magician. But just before she could grab the lamp, he spun around and seized her. He cast a terrible spell. Bala found herself trapped in an hourglass!

"Admit you love me and I'll let you go!" the magician promised.

Never. Ever.

Ever

EVER!

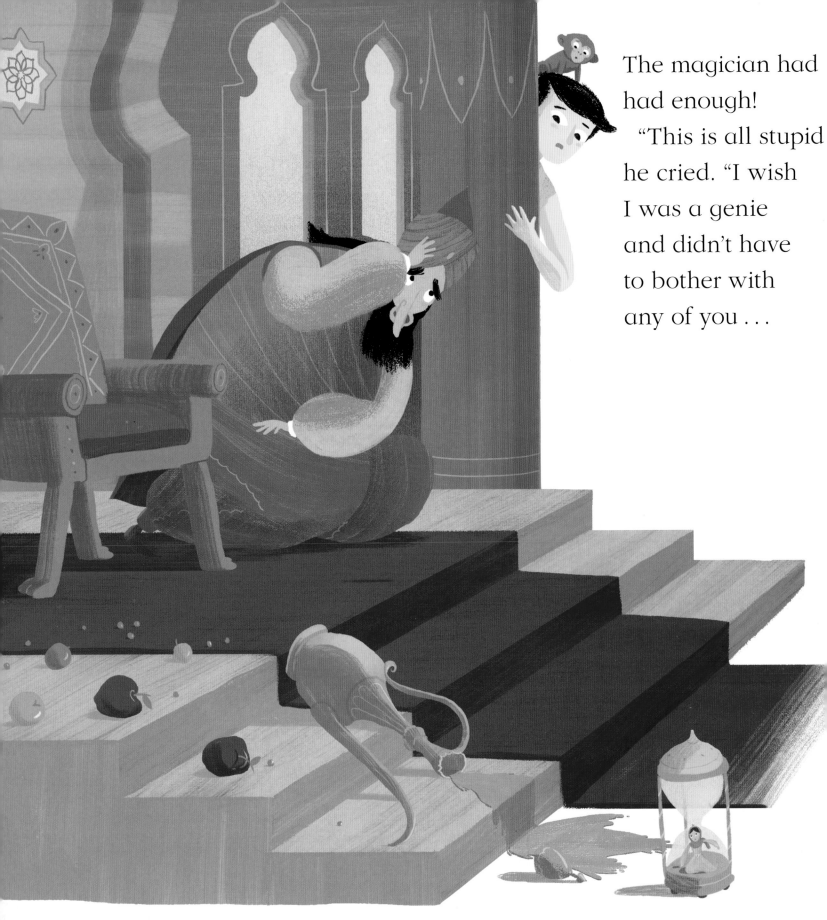

The magician had had enough!
"This is all stupid he cried. "I wish I was a genie and didn't have to bother with any of you . . .

Oh . . .
dear . . .
I just used my **final wish!**"

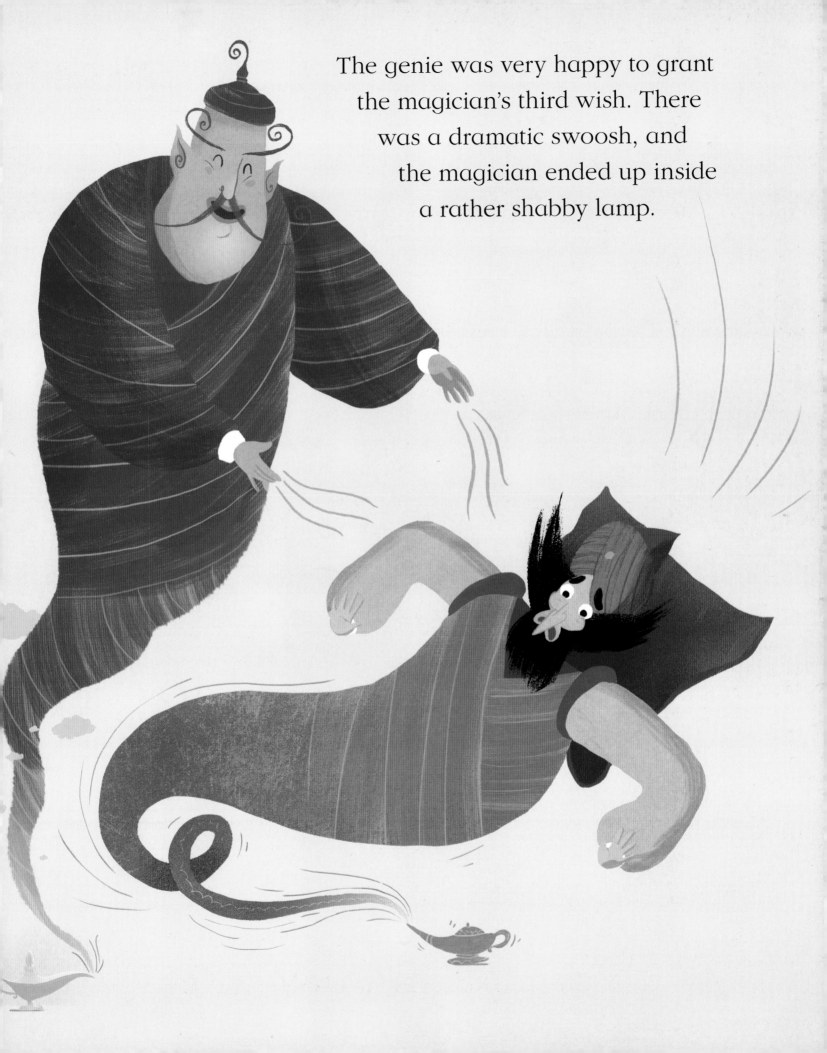

The genie was very happy to grant
the magician's third wish. There
was a dramatic swoosh, and
the magician ended up inside
a rather shabby lamp.

When the magician was gone, the hourglass shattered. Bala was free!

"If only I was a prince then I could marry you," said Aladdin.

"So use your third wish!" said Bala.

"I can't," Aladdin sighed. "I need that for something else. Genie, I wish you were free!"

The delighted genie flowed out of his lamp and disappeared.

Bala turned to the sultan. "See! Aladdin is brave *and* kind. You must let me marry him."

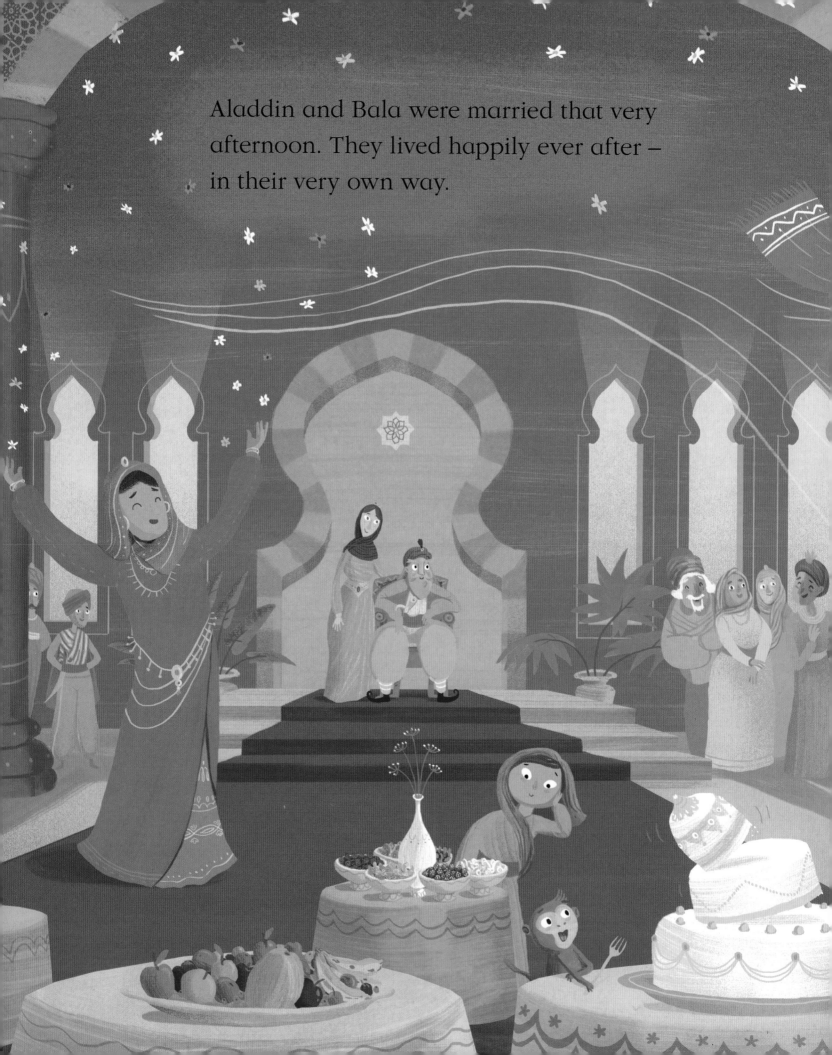

Aladdin and Bala were married that very afternoon. They lived happily ever after – in their very own way.

FAIRYTALE CLASSICS

are familiar, fun and friendly stories –
with a marvellously modern twist!

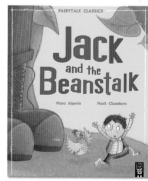

For information regarding any of the above titles or for our catalogue, please contact us:
Little Tiger Press Ltd, 1 Coda Studios, 189 Munster Road, London SW6 6AW
Tel: 020 7385 6333 • E-mail: contact@littletiger.co.uk • www.littletiger.co.uk